An historical introduction to the European Union

An Historical Introduction to the European Union by Philip Thody is a chronological political history of European integration from the Common Market to the present with a contextualising survey of wider European history since the 1600s. This accessible introduction to the essential history, economics and politics of the European Union offers a clear survey of the Union up to the present day.

With a detailed account of the workings of the Union, this book includes discussion of enlargement, organisations and powers, the basic principles behind the Union, contested practices such as agriculture, legislation and monetary policy.

Incorporating the most recent research, this book includes detailed treatment of the policies of the European Union as well as a chronology and guide to the institutions of the European Union and suggestions for further reading.

Philip Thody is Emeritus Professor at Leeds University and author of *The Conservative Imagination* and *French Caesarism from Napoleon I to Charles de Gaulle*.

An historical introduction to the European Union

Philip Thody

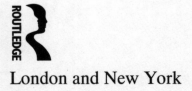

London and New York

First published 1997
by Routledge
11 New Fetter Lane, London EC4P 4EE

Simultaneously published in the USA and Canada
by Routledge
29 West 35th Street, New York, NY 10001

© 1997 Philip Thody

Typeset in Times by
Ponting–Green Publishing Services, Chesham, Buckinghamshire

Printed and bound in Great Britain by
Clays Ltd, St Ives PLC

British Library Cataloguing in Publication Data
A catalogue record for this book is available from the
British Library

Library of Congress Cataloguing in Publication Data
A catalogue record for this book has been requested

ISBN 0–415–17107–5

To Jim Walsh

Contents

Acknowledgement

I am particularly grateful to my friend and former colleague Howard Evans for all his help and advice in preparing this book. Any mistakes are mine; but they would be much more numerous if Howard had not read the typescript with such exemplary care.

Chronology

This historical *aide-mémoire* has two aims: to provide a checklist for the events mentioned in the text, and especially in Chapter 1; and to offer a reminder of the international climate against which the European Coal and Steel Community (ECSC) has developed into the European Union.

1950

9 May   In a speech inspired by Jean Monnet the French Foreign Minister, Robert Schuman, proposes that France and the Federal Republic of Germany should join together in pooling their iron and steel resources, and invites other European countries to join them.

2 June   In response to an invitation to involve itself in the Schuman initiative, the United Kingdom announces that it will not take part in talks aimed at the creation of an organisation which will require states to accept the authority of a supra-national body.

20 June   Talks begin in Paris among the six countries which have accepted the Schuman invitation – Belgium, France, the Federal Republic of Germany, Italy, Luxembourg and the Netherlands. Negotiations begin with a view to establishing the ECSC.

24 June   Troops from Communist North Korea invade South Korea. Troops from the United States, Australia, Belgium, Great Britain, France, New Zealand, Turkey and nine other countries fight under the flag of the United Nations to defend South Korea. An armistice is signed on 27 July 1953 re-establishing the border between North and South Korea on the 38th parallel. There is widespread feeling in Western Europe that a comparable invasion to the one which took place in Korea in June could carry Soviet-backed armies to the Channel ports in less than a week, and might well do so if the West were to show the slightest sign of weakness. It is this feeling which lies behind the attempt to create the European Defence Community (EDC) in 1952.

1951

18 April   Belgium, France, the Federal Republic of Germany, Italy, Luxembourg and the Netherlands sign the Treaty of Paris establishing the ECSC.

1952

17 May   Belgium, France, Italy, the Federal Republic of Germany, Luxembourg and the Netherlands sign the Treaty of Paris establishing the EDC. The project is strongly supported by the United States of America, but has to be ratified by the parliaments of each member state. All except France agree, with the French parliament finally rejecting the proposal on 30 August 1954, by 319 votes to 264.

15 July   After having been ratified by all six national parliaments, the Treaty of Paris establishing the ECSC comes into force. Luxembourg is chosen as the provisional site for the headquarters of the High Authority responsible for administering it.

1953

10 February   In accordance with the Treaty of Paris of 18 April 1951, a common market comes into force for coal and iron ore. No customs duties are imposed on these products as they are bought and sold by firms in the six member countries of the ECSC, and no individual country has the right to limit the amount or quality of these products entering or leaving its territory.

1 May   A similar common market comes into force for steel. The quantity of steel produced by the firms in all six countries, like the tonnage and quality of coal extracted, gradually comes under the control of the Luxembourg authorities, which consult with the member states as to the best policy to be followed.

26–28 November A joint meeting of cabinet ministers from the six member countries of the ECSC establishes an intergovernmental conference to draw up plans for a treaty establishing a European economic community.

1954

20–23 October After the rejection of the European Defence Community by the French parliament on 30 August 1954, an intergovernmental meeting is held in London to establish the Western European Union (WEU). This groups together Belgium, France, Spain, Germany, Italy, Portugal, Luxembourg, the Netherlands and the United Kingdom, in order to co-ordinate the defence of Western Europe. It is supported by the United States, which sees it as a step towards the admission of the Federal Republic of Germany into the North Atlantic Treaty Organisation (NATO) established on 4 April 1949, and whose first members were Belgium, Canada, Denmark, France, Iceland, Italy, Luxembourg, the Netherlands, Norway, Portugal, the United Kingdom and the United States. Like NATO, the WEU is acceptable to the United Kingdom because it is an alliance of a traditional type between sovereign states. It is under the auspices of the WEU that the United Kingdom agrees to keep two brigades of troops on the continent of Europe for a period of twenty-five years in the first instance, thus helping to prepare France to accept the entry of the Federal Republic of Germany into NATO in 1955.

1955

1–2 June At the Messina conference, at which the United Kingdom is invited to participate, the Foreign Ministers of the six member states of the ECSC decide to extend the process of European integration to the whole of their economies. A committee is set up, under the chairmanship of the Belgian Foreign Minister Paul-Henri Spaak, to examine the possibility of a general European economic community, together with co-operation in the development of atomic energy.

1956

29–30 May Representatives of the six member governments of the ECSC

decide to follow the recommendations of the Spaak committee and conduct negotiations with a view to establishing a
European Economic Community (EEC) and a European
Atomic Energy Community (Euratom). Further negotiations
aimed at establishing both communities, and at organising
co-operation between them, open in Brussels on 26 June.

17 July   The United Kingdom, made conscious by the decisions
stemming from the Messina conference that co-operation on
the lines of the ECSC would involve an unacceptable loss of
sovereignty, decides to set up a working party under the
auspices of the Organisation for European Economic Co-
operation (OEEC) in order to create a European Free Trade
Association (EFTA), a rival organisation which will differ
from the proposed EEC by not being a customs union, with
a common tariff separating its members from the rest of the
world, but simply a free trade zone in which countries abolish
tariffs between themselves.

26 July   Colonel Nasser announces the nationalisation of the Suez
Canal. The objections of Great Britain and France finally take
the form of a military intervention against Egypt, carried out
on 31 October 1956, ostensibly to 'separate the combatants'
after the Israeli attack on Egypt on 29 October. Under the
combined pressure of the United States of America and the
USSR, British and French forces agree to a ceasefire on 6
November, two days after the armed forces of the Soviet
Union have intervened in Hungary to prevent that country
leaving the Warsaw pact, established in 1955 in response to
NATO under the auspices of the USSR. The French, who
would have liked to go on with the campaign against Egypt
until Colonel Nasser was forced to resign, feel badly let down
by the British, a fact which may lie in part behind de Gaulle's
rejection of the British application for membership of the
EEC in 1963 and again in 1967.

1957

25 March   The six member countries of the ECSC sign the Treaty of
Rome, establishing the EEC and Euratom. The aim of the
Treaty of Rome is to create a community; establish a
common market by the removal of obstacles to the free
movement of capital, goods, people and services; to establish
a common external trade policy and common agricultural,

fisheries and transport policies; to co-ordinate economic policies, harmonise social policies; and to co-operate in nuclear research for peaceful purposes. Between July and November, this treaty is ratified by the parliaments of the six member countries.

1958

1 January   The Treaty of Rome comes into force, with the headquarters of the EEC and Euratom Commissions being established in Brussels, and the other institutions of the EEC and Euratom at Strasbourg and Luxembourg.

3–11 July   The Stresa conference agrees on the principles governing the Common Agricultural Policy (CAP): market support; community preference; financial help for exports; and a common external tariff.

3 September   Success of de Gaulle in the referendum to establish the Fifth Republic, which comes into force on 1 January 1959.

28 November   Soviet note informing France, Great Britain and the United States of the intention of the Soviet Union to sign a separate peace treaty with the German Democratic Republic on 28 May 1959. The implied threat to the independence of West Berlin is a reminder of the Berlin blockade of June 1948 – May 1949, and leads to a series of political crises and confrontations between the Soviet Union and the NATO powers.

1959

1 January   First reduction, 10 per cent, in customs duties on manufactured goods between the six member states of the EEC, and first reduction, 20 per cent, of import and export quotas.

1960

1 January   Second reduction, 10 per cent, in import and export quotas.

4 January   Signature of treaty establishing European Free Trade Area (EFTA), grouping together Austria, Denmark, Norway, Portugal, Sweden, Switzerland and the United Kingdom. This treaty comes into force on 1 July.

11 May   Establishment of the European Social Fund.

12 May   The Council of Ministers decides to move more quickly in implementing the provisions of the Treaty of Rome.

1 July   Second reduction, 10 per cent, in customs duties.

1961

1 January   Third reduction, 10 per cent, in customs duties; third reduction, 10 per cent, in import and export quotas.

10–11 February The Foreign Ministers of the six member countries of the EEC make a formal statement of support for a European political union.

18 July   The Heads of State of the six member states meet in Bonn and declare their support for the 'creation of a union of European states'.

31 July   The Republic of Ireland, a neutral state not belonging to NATO, the WEU or EFTA, applies for admission to the EEC.

9–10 August   The United Kingdom and Denmark announce that they are applying for membership of the EEC. Negotiations begin in November.

13 August   The authorities of the German Democratic Republic close the border between their section of the city and West Berlin; and begin to build a wall preventing their citizens travelling to the West.

1962

1 January   Fourth reduction, 10 per cent, in customs duties.

14 January   Agreement on the form to be taken by the CAP, which for cereals, eggs, fruit, pig meat, poultry and vegetables comes into force on 30 July.

1 July   Fifth reduction, 10 per cent, in customs duties.

1 July   End of the Algerian war. Algeria, an integral part of France since 1848, becomes an independent country.

20 October   The United States announces that it has evidence that the USSR is installing medium-range nuclear missiles in Cuba, and blockades the island to prevent further material from arriving. On 26 October, the USSR agrees to withdraw its missiles.

1963

14 January   General de Gaulle announces at a press conference that Great Britain, a country with 'a maritime and insular destiny', is not ready to become a member of the EEC, and that France will therefore veto her application for membership.

1 July   Sixth reduction, 10 per cent, in customs duties.

18 July   Signature of the first Yaoundé convention with eighteen countries from Africa and the Pacific, giving them preferential treatment in the application of the common external tariff to some of their agricultural products.

16–23 December   A series of long meetings in Brussels finally reaches agreement on the extension of the CAP to beef, milk and milk products and rice.

1964

2 May   An alleged attack on United States ships in the Gulf of Tonkin leads to progressive United States involvement in the Vietnam War. This involvement does not end until 27 January 1973, when United States forces begin to withdraw. On 9 November 1975, Vietnam is united under Communist rule from the North. The refusal of the United States government to increase taxes to pay for the war, and its consequent need to issue more dollars, is seen as a major factor in the suspension of the convertibility of the dollar into gold in August 1971.

1965

1 January   Seventh reduction, 10 per cent, in customs duties.

8 April   Signature of a treaty merging the executives of the three Communities (the EEC, the ECSC and Euratom). This treaty comes into effect on 1 July 1967.

30 June   France rejects the Hallstein Plan, named after the first President of the European Commission, aimed at enabling more and more of the duties levied under the common external tariff to be transferred to the Community, thus creating an independent community budget. For seven months, France holds up all progress in the EEC by implementing the 'empty chair' policy whereby its representatives do not attend meetings.

1966

1 January   Eighth reduction, 10 per cent, in customs duties.

1 January   Adoption of the 'Luxembourg compromise' whereby a member state of the EEC is allowed to veto a proposal if it considers that its 'vital national interests' are affected. The acceptance of this compromise allows France to resume participation in meetings of the EEC committees, and marks a triumph for the Gaullist concept of 'l'Europe des Patries', a Europe of sovereign nation states, over a federal Europe preferred by the Federal Republic of Germany and the Benelux countries of Belgium, the Netherlands and Luxembourg.

10 November The Labour Prime Minister, Harold Wilson, announces that his government will re-apply for membership of the EEC.

1967

1 January   Ninth reduction, 5 per cent, in customs duties.

10 May   The United Kingdom, Denmark and Ireland re-apply for admission to the EEC, followed on 21 July by Norway.

10–16 June   Israel, threatened by an apparently imminent invasion by Syria and Egypt, strikes first, wins a series of victories, and occupies the Sinai Desert, the Golan Heights and the city of Jerusalem.

3–6 July   First meeting of the European Commission as the body now responsible for the EEC, the ECSC and Euratom, now known as the European Communities.

27 November General de Gaulle again vetoes the British application for membership of the EEC.

18–19   A meeting in Brussels of the Heads of State and Govern-
December   ment of the six member countries of the EEC officially admit their disagreement on the enlargement of the Community, France being the only country unwilling to accept the United Kingdom as a member.

1968

May   French workers and trade unions join student protesters in Paris and elsewhere and begin a national strike. They are persuaded to go back to work by the 'accords de Grenelle' of 27 May which grant large wage increases, improved working conditions and better pension arrangements. The events of May 1968 affect the development of the EEC in two ways: had de Gaulle's confidence in himself not been shaken, he would not have called and lost the referendum of April 1969, would not have been replaced by Georges Pompidou, and the entry of the United Kingdom into the European Community would have been postponed for a further two years; without the inflationary effects of the Grenelle agreements, the sudden devaluation of the French franc on 10 August 1969 would not have sparked off the monetary instability which inspired the first attempts at European Monetary Union (EMU).

1 July   Abolition, eighteen months ahead of the timetable originally agreed in 1957, of all customs duties on manufactured goods between the six member states of the EEC, and introduction of the common external tariff.

1969

28 April   De Gaulle loses the referendum on regional reform and reform of the Senate, resigns as President of the Fifth Republic.

15 June   Election as President of Georges Pompidou.

10 August   Sudden devaluation by 6.6 per cent of the French franc, followed by revaluation of 2 per cent of the Deutschmark and the Dutch guilder.

1–2 December   At a summit meeting in the Hague, the six member governments of the EEC agree to bring the transitional period officially to an end, to make permanent the arrangements already in force for the CAP, and to move towards an arrangement whereby the Community will have its own resources and will thus no longer depend exclusively on financial contributions made by the member states. France thus begins to abandon the rigidly nationalistic position adopted in 1965 under General de Gaulle, and Georges Pompidou suggests that future negotiations for the entry of the United Kingdom into the EEC are likely to succeed.

1971

23 March   A farmer is killed during a demonstration in Brussels against the implementation of the plan proposed in December 1969 by Sicco Mansholt whereby small farms would gradually be replaced by much larger, more economically efficient farms on the American and Canadian models. By 1982, the gradual adoption of this plan will lead to a reduction of the number of people working on the land in the EEC from 20 per cent to just under 8 per cent, accompanied by an average increase in production of 2 per cent a year.

19 May   Introduction of Monetary Compensation Payments to protect German and Dutch agriculture against what is seen as unfair competition created by the loss in value of the French franc and the Italian lira.

10 August President Nixon suspends the convertibility of the dollar.

28 October Acceptance by the British Parliament, by 356 votes to 244, with 22 abstentions, of the entry of the United Kingdom into the EEC on the conditions negotiated by the Conservative Prime Minister, Edward Heath. The Labour Leader, Harold Wilson, makes it clear that his party will renegotiate these conditions when it comes to power.

1972

22 January Denmark, Ireland, Norway and the United Kingdom sign the treaty making them members of the EEC. In a referendum held on 26 September, the Norwegians decide not to join.

23 April   A referendum in France gives a 'Yes' vote of 67 per cent in favour of the enlargement of the EEC.

24 April   In order to provide more stability between the value of their currencies, the six member states of the EEC agree to limit the extent to which they can vary with respect to the dollar to 2.5 per cent. This arrangement is popularly referred to as the 'snake in the tunnel', and can be seen as a first step towards a common or single currency.

1973

1 January Official entry of the United Kingdom, Denmark and Ireland into the EEC, with a transitional period of five years.

6 October Yom Kippour, Egypt and Syria attack Israel. On 25 October, the USSR announces that it will supplement its diplomatic support and provision of arms for Egypt and Syria by the despatch of 200,000 airborne troops to prevent the Israelis from annihilating the Egyptian third army, which they have surrounded. The United States discourages this move by putting its nuclear forces on full alert, and both the Israelis and the Soviets refrain from further action. Before a ceasefire is agreed on 4 November, the Organisation of Petroleum Producing Countries (OPEC), most of whose members are allies of Egypt and who are more representative of the Arab, Moslem world than of any other grouping, say that they will refuse to sell oil to any country which supports Israel. This leads the Dutch government to make 4 November 1973 'a carless day', and to a widespread feeling that this is the end of our civilisation as we know it. The OPEC countries finally restrict themselves to quadrupling the price of oil, and there is a further sharp rise after the fall of the Shah of Iran in 1979 and his eventual replacement by the militantly Islamic régime of the Ayotallah Khomeini. With the Middle East supplying at the time two-thirds of the world's supply of oil, the OPEC countries are able to increase the price of oil by 475 per cent between 1 January 1973 and 1 January 1979.

1974

1 April First reduction, 40 per cent, in the customs duties of the three new members in the transitional period bring their rates into line with those of the Common External Tariff.

2 April The Labour government of Harold Wilson, elected on 28 February, requests a renegotiation of the entry conditions for the United Kingdom into the EEC.

9–10 December At a summit meeting in Paris, the nine Heads of State and Government decide to meet three times a year on a regular basis in what is to be known as the European Council (not to be confused with the Council of the European Communities, the main decision-making body of the EEC, the ECSC and Euratom) or the Council of Europe. The Heads of State and Government also decide to organise direct elections to the European Parliament, and to establish the European Regional Development Fund.

12 December For the first time, the European Parliament votes to approve the Community budget.

1975

28 February Signature of the first Lomé Convention between the European Communities and 46 states in Africa and the Pacific. This enables Britain and France to maintain contact with their former colonies and 99 per cent of the agricultural exports of these countries enter the EEC at guaranteed prices without paying the Common External Tariff.

5 June   Sixty-seven per cent of those voting in the referendum held in Great Britain on the new terms negotiated by the Labour government approve British membership of the EEC.

22 July   Signature of a treaty establishing the Court of Auditors, which will begin work on 1 June 1977, and giving the European Parliament wider budgetary powers.

1976

7 July   Official beginning of negotiations for the entry of Greece into the EEC.

1977

1 January   Establishment of a fishing zone of 200 maritime miles around the coasts of the member states, to which boats from Community countries will all have equal access.

28 March   Portugal applies for membership of the EEC; followed on 28 July by Spain.

31 December End of the transitional period allowed to the United Kingdom, Denmark and Ireland to bring their agricultural prices in line with those of the other member states.

1978

6–7 July   At the meeting of the European Council held in Bremen, France and the Federal Republic of Germany present a scheme for closer monetary co-operation, involving the creation of the European Monetary System (EMS) to replace the 'snake in the tunnel'.

17 October Beginning of negotiations for the entry of Portugal.

1979

13 March   Introduction of the EMS. The value of the European Currency Unit (ECU) is based on the relationship between a basket of European currencies and the United States dollar. Its present value is 0.8376 of £1.

7–10 June   First direct elections to the European Parliament, which now has 410 members. Except in the United Kingdom, the system adopted is one of proportional representation. Sixty per cent of the total European electorate votes, and the largest single party is a socialist coalition.

19–30 November At the Dublin summit, Mrs Thatcher, in power since May 1979, demands a reduction in the British contribution to the European budget.

13 December For the first time, the European Parliament rejects the budget, by 288 votes to 64, in the hope of bringing about a reform of the CAP.

20 December At its annual meeting, NATO decides to counter the installation of Soviet SS20 medium range nuclear missiles in Eastern Europe by the placing of United States Cruise and Pershing missiles in the United Kingdom, Italy and West Germany.

24 December Forty thousand Soviet troops move into Afghanistan in order to support the Marxist government against a nationalistic rebellion by fundamentalist Moslems.

1980

10 October A combination of over-production and a decline in demand having led to a serious crisis in the steel industry, the Council of Ministers, in accordance with the Treaty of Paris of 1951, officially declares that the ECSC is in a state of crisis and establishes quotas limiting production in all nine countries of the Communities.

1981

1 January Greece becomes the tenth member of the EEC.

10 May François Mitterrand is elected President of the French Republic, and the legislative elections of June give an overall majority to the socialist party for the first time in the history of the Fifth Republic.

4 October The attempt of the French government to cure unemployment by a programme of public investment and increased wages leads to a decline of the value of the franc. Together with the Italian lira, it is officially devalued by 3 per cent in the EMS, while the value of the Deutschmark and Dutch guilder is increased by 5.5 per cent.

1982

12 June   The pursuit of Keynesian reflationary policies in France
                having led to a further value in the decline of the franc, the
                value of the Deutschmark and Dutch guilder is increased by
                4.5 per cent in the EMS, while that of the franc and lira is
                reduced by a further 2.75 per cent.

1983

21 March   The value of the franc in the EMS is further reduced, this
                time by 2.5 per cent; that of the lira and the Irish punt by
                3.5 per cent. The value of the Deutschmark is increased
                by 5.5 per cent, that of the Dutch guilder by 3.5 per cent,
                of the Danish krøner by 2.5 per cent and of the Belgian
                franc by 1.5 per cent.

1984

28 February Adoption of the Esprit programme for research in informa-
                tion technology.
9 April   Opening at Culham, near Oxford, of the Joint European
                Tours (JET) research institute and laboratories, as part of a
                programme of research in the peaceful use of atomic energy
                financed by Euratom.
24 May   In a speech to the European parliament, François Mitterrand
                calls for the development of a common European defence
                policy and comments on the widespread movement of protest
                against the installation of Cruise and Pershing missiles that
                'the pacifists are in the West, but the missiles are in the East'.
                However, since France has not been a member of the NATO
                command structure since 1966, there are no Cruise or
                Pershings on French soil.
June   At the Fontainebleau summit, the European Council reaches
                agreement on the United Kingdom budget contribution.
17–24 June Second direct elections of the 434 members of the European
                Parliament. This meets for the first time later in the month
                in Strasbourg. Its administrative offices are in Luxembourg
                and its committees meet in Brussels.

1985

1 January   The new European Commission begins its five-year period of office. Jacques Delors, having resigned as French Finance Minister, is elected President, and will be re-elected in 1990.
2–4   At its meeting in Luxembourg, the European Council adopts
December   the Single European Act and sets the date of 1 January 1993 for completion of the Single Market.

1986

1 January   Spain and Portugal join the EEC. The population of the 12 member states is now 321 million.
17 February Signature of the Single European Act, which comes into force on 1 July 1987 and codifies the mutual recognition of qualifications, the open tendering for public works contracts, the free movement of capital, moves towards the harmonisation of Value Added Tax (VAT) and excise duties, and the reduction of state aid to individual industries. It also introduces more voting by a qualified majority in the Council of Ministers and increases the powers of the European Parliament.

1987

14 April   Turkey applies to join the Community.
27 October   At its conference in the Hague, the WEU adopts a joint security programme.

1988

February   At a meeting in Brussels chaired by Chancellor Kohl, the European Council agrees to a reform of the CAP, to the need for a balanced Community budget and a reform of the Structural Funds.
15 September At a speech in Bruges, Mrs Thatcher attacks the move towards a federal and socialist Europe which she sees as represented by Jacques Delors, and urges the maintenance of a Europe based on independent nation states and free market economics. President Mitterrand, in contrast, argues that the free movement of capital is impossible without a strengthening of the EMS.

1989

7 February   Jacques Delors presents his report on economic and monetary union, recommending three stages in the creation of the Single Currency due to come into existence on 1 January 1999: a strengthening of existing co-operation on exchange rates, the creation of a federation of European banks, and the establishment of fixed exchange rates.

9 November   The East German authorities suddenly allow free passage of their citizens through the Berlin Wall, first erected on 13 August 1961. The fact that they have been allowed to do so by the Soviet authorities marks the end of the Cold War in Europe, and will lead to German re-unification on 3 October 1990. The West has won the Cold War, though it immediately becomes unfashionable to say so. One reason for this is that the German Federal Republic now has to devote much of the economic strength which enabled it to make the European Community a success into rebuilding the economy of the former German Democratic Republic.

12 December   At the meeting of the European Council in Strasbourg, eleven of the twelve member states of the European Community adopt the Social Chapter, with the United Kingdom declining to take part. The twelve agree that conditions are ripe for an inter-governmental conference on economic and monetary union, to be held before the end of 1990.

1990

11 May   Signature in Bonn of a treaty of monetary union between the German Federal Republic and the former German Democratic Republic.

19 June   France, Germany and the three Benelux countries sign the Schengen Convention abolishing passport controls at their internal frontiers. Italy, Spain and Portugal subsequently join the 'Schengen group'. However, due to delays in providing the necessary computer technology for tracking terrorists and known criminals, together, in France, with the fear of a massive influx of illegal immigrants, the convention has still to be fully implemented.

3 October   German reunification.

5 October   The United Kingdom joins the European Exchange

Rate Mechanism (ERM), with the pound fixed at 2.93 Deutschmark.

1991

11 December Signature of the Maastricht Treaty on European Union, defining the three pillars on which European unification will henceforth be based: the European Community, in the form it has reached in 1991; the development of a common foreign and security policy, to be agreed by the Council of Ministers, which thus takes on an expanded role; co-operation on justice and interior affairs, again with the Council of Ministers co-ordinating policies on asylum, immigration, cross-border crime, conditions of entry, drug trafficking and international terrorism.

1992

2 June The Danish referendum on the Maastricht Treaty gives a 'No' vote. This casts doubt on the feasibility of the plans for economic and monetary union, and adds to the general uncertainty in the money markets.

16 September On 'Black Wednesday', the pound is forced to leave the ERM, and falls to 2.25 Deutschmark. This is considered a much more realistic rate, and the devaluation which it represents gives rise to an apparent improvement in the United Kingdom's economic performance. Exports rise, and by 1996 unemployment falls to 7.6 per cent of the working population, as opposed to 12 per cent in France and over 13 per cent in Germany. By April 1997, however, the pound is back at 2.83 Deutschmark.

20 September In a closely contested referendum, France narrowly accepts the Maastricht Treaty, and in a second referendum, held on 18 May 1993, the Danes change their mind and say 'Yes' as well.

31 December The single internal market programme is officially completed.

1993

August Further movements in the international money markets lead to the effective suspension of the ERM as the official bands in which European currencies are allowed to fluctuate expand from the narrow band of 2.25 per cent, through to a medium band of 6 per cent, or, if they wish, to 15 per cent.

1 November   The Maastricht Treaty officially comes into force, establishing the European Union.

1994

1 January   Establishment of the European Economic Area by closer co-operation between the remaining members of EFTA with the countries of the European Union.

1995

1 January   Austria, Finland and Sweden become members of the European Union.

1 July   Official entry into force of the Schengen agreements on the abolition of frontier controls.

1996

3 September   At a meeting in Bonn, Jacques Chirac and François Mitterrand insist that moves will go ahead to introduce a single currency on 1 January 1999, in spite of the harm which the *franc fort* policy (keeping the franc at the same level as the Deutschmark) is said to be doing to the French economy.

December   At its meeting in Madrid, the European Council confirms its intention of going ahead with the introduction of the European Single Currency on 1 January 1999.

1997

May–June   While the election of a Labour government in Great Britain on 1 May seems to increase the chances of European Unification, the victory of the French socialists in the legislative elections of 25 May and 1 June looks initially as though it might prove an obstacle to the proposed creation of a Single Currency on 1 January 1999. At the Amersterdam summit of 15–17 June, a compromise is apparently reached between the French desire to devote resources to the reduction of unemployment, and the German insistence on the strict observance of the monetarist criteria originally agreed at Maastricht in 1993.

1   History

COAL, STEEL AND SOVEREIGNTY

The European Union has its origins in the European Coal and Steel Community (ECSC), established on 18 April 1951 by the Treaty of Paris. The immediate political aim of the ECSC was to avoid the risk of future conflict between France and Germany by linking the two basic elements in their economies, the production of coal and the manufacture of steel, more closely together. In 1870, the hostility between France and Germany had led to the only major European war to take place between the end of the Napoleonic wars in 1815 and the beginning of the first world war ninety-nine years later. Between 1914 and 1918, this hostility had been a major factor in the first world war, and a contributory cause of the second. The best way to avoid a fourth conflict, it was argued, was to tie the economies of the two countries so closely together that it would become physically impossible for them ever to fight each other again. In so far as it is now inconceivable that a war should break out between France and Germany – or, indeed, between any of the fifteen countries making up what is now known as the European Union[1] – its first political aim has been totally achieved.

The initial proposal to establish the ECSC had been made on 9 May 1950 by the French Foreign Minister, Robert Schuman, and enthusiastically accepted by the Chancellor of the German Federal Republic, Konrad Adenauer. The French and Germans then invited other Western European countries to join them, and their invitation was taken up by Belgium, Italy, Luxembourg and the Netherlands. These were all countries which saw in the creation of the ECSC the possibility of linking their own economies to those of Western Europe's two largest nations, while at the same time helping to avoid yet another war. Schuman himself had been born in Luxembourg in 1886 of a French-speaking family from Lorraine, one of the two provinces taken from France by Germany after the French defeat in the war of 1870, and had been forced to serve in the German army during the

1914–1918 war. After 1918, when France recovered Lorraine and its sister province of Alsace, he officially became a French citizen again, but remained acutely and understandably aware of the need for Franco-German reconciliation.

The two countries had been in conflict since the sixteenth century, when the rivalry between Francis I of France and Charles V, King of Spain and Holy Roman Emperor, led to fighting in the south of France and in Italy, as well as to an alliance, in 1536, between Catholic France and the then militantly Islamic Turkey. In the seventeenth century, France deliberately prolonged the Thirty Years War of 1618–1648 in order to weaken the House of Austria, which then had authority over much of what is now Germany, and the armies of Louis XIV laid waste the Palatinate. In the early nineteenth century, Napoleon I had defeated and humiliated Austria and Prussia, before being defeated himself by an army containing Austrian and Prussian soldiers as well as British and Russian ones. Later on, once Prussia had defeated Austria in the war of 1867, it was obvious to Bismarck that the best way to unify Germany behind Prussian leadership was to provoke a war against France. This he did, on 18 July 1870, and in January 1871, after the defeat of France, the Prussians signed the treaty in the Hall of Mirrors at Versailles which marked the beginning of the Second Reich, the régime which governed Germany until the defeat of 1918 led to its being replaced by the Weimar Republic of 1919–1933.

The Germans had economic as well as political reasons for insisting in 1870 on taking away the two provinces of Alsace and Lorraine and making them an integral part of their newly unified country. Lorraine was rich in deposits of iron ore, which the Germans could combine with the coal of the Ruhr basin to make their steel industry the largest in continental Europe, and this industry was soon to overtake that of the United Kingdom. One of the principal aims of France during the first world war, from 1914–1918, had been to recover what she had never ceased to think of as her national territory. The Treaty of Versailles, in 1919, had done this, but the defeat of 1940 saw Alsace and Lorraine, together with parts of northern France, incorporated into Hitler's Third Reich in the same way as they had been into the Second Reich of Kaiser Wilhelm II between 1870 and 1919. Germany's defeat in 1945 led to the two provinces going back to France again, but Robert Schuman was not the only European statesman to feel that the enmity between France and Germany, the root cause of the first world war, ought to come to an end.

It was the businessman, economist and political thinker, Jean Monnet, who dedicated his life after the second world war to the creation of what he, like Churchill, called 'the United States of Europe', who had originally suggested to Robert Schuman the idea of beginning with the two basic industries of coal and steel. In the 1950s, 70 per cent of the energy needs of Western Europe were met by coal, and no country could have an effective army without steel. If the coal mines and steel mills of France and Germany were brought under international control, Monnet argued, it would become physically impossible for the two countries to go to war with each other again, and Robert Schuman agreed. The British, however, for reasons discussed below, did not accept the invitation to become one of the founder members of the organisation which was eventually, in 1991, to give birth to the European Union.

The ECSC proved as successful in its immediate economic objectives as it was to be in its long-term political aims. It gave the French access to the rich coal deposits of the Ruhr, and ended the dual pricing system whereby German coal bought for the steel mills of Lorraine cost 46 per cent more than the same coal burnt in West Germany.[2] It removed all customs barriers to the sale of coal and steel among the six participating countries so much so that by 1958, and the end of the transitional period allowed for in the Treaty of Paris of April 1951, interstate trading in steel between the six member countries had increased by 151 per cent, that of coal by 21 per cent and that of iron ore by 25 per cent. Since the 1970s, the problem has been more that of managing the decline in these two traditional industries, and the Chronology has a note on how this problem was dealt with in 1980. What was more immediately important, in the context of the general movement towards European unification which has been such a marked feature of the last fifty years, was the model offered by the ECSC, and the way it enabled other problems to be, if not solved, at least circumvented.

Politically, it was to provide the starting point for the European Economic Community (EEC) of 1958, with the individual states agreeing to hand over the management of important sections of what had previously been seen as their national economy in accordance with Directives issued by a supra-national body, the High Authority. This consisted of nine members, holding office for six years. Eight of them were designated by the governments of the Six, with one extra member being chosen by the eight who had already been appointed. This Authority had the right to decide on prices and levels of production, and offered favourable conditions which enabled, for example, the Belgian coal industry to be subsidised by Germany and Holland, and Italy to have access to coal mined in French North Africa.

The establishment of the ECSC also removed another source of inter-national friction by enabling the Saarland to be integrated into what was increasingly a combined European operation for the production of coal and steel. After 1919, the Treaty of Versailles had declared Germany guilty of having started the first world war and placed one of its major industrial areas, the Saarland, under the control of the newly-established League of Nations, entrusting the management of its coal industry to the French. This caused considerable resentment among the Germans, and the decision by plebiscite of the Saarlanders, in 1935, to go back to Germany was felt in France as a serious political defeat. A similar decision to place the Saarland under international control was taken at the end of the second world war, in 1945, but the Saarlanders were again to decide by plebiscite, in January 1957, to become part of Germany again. This time, however, because the production of coal and steel was becoming a European affair in which decisions were no longer taken by nation states for obviously nationalist reasons, the French reaction was much more muted.

POLITICS, NATIONALISM AND DEFENCE

A series of events which took place elsewhere in Europe immediately after the signature of the Treaty of Paris in April 1951 suggested that the British might have made a sensible decision to keep out when they declined the invitation to join the ECSC as founder members with Belgium, France, West Germany, Italy, Luxembourg and the Netherlands. They did so for a number of reasons, the first of which was summarised by Clement Attlee, Labour Prime Minister from 1945 to 1951, when he said that we were 'not going to join a group of nations in which we have just saved four of them from the other two', and at the time, his remark was fully understandable.

In 1940, only eleven years before the establishment of the ECSC, the Germans had been bombing Great Britain and preparing to invade. The French Third Republic (1871–1940) had collapsed, and signed an armistice which involved, in the words of Marshal Pétain, the official Head of State of the Vichy régime which replaced it, a policy of collaboration with Nazi Germany. The Dutch had tried, unsuccessfully, to stay neutral; the Belgians had not proved reliable allies; while the Italians, under the leadership of Mussolini, had waited until the French and British armies had been defeated before declaring war on them on 10 June 1940. The Australians, Canadians and New Zealanders, in contrast, had been in the war against Germany from the beginning to the end. Once the Japanese had attacked them at Pearl Harbour on Sunday 7 December 1941, and Hitler fulfilled his obligations as an Axis power by declaring war on the United States, the Americans had pursued the war against Germany with vigour, and given priority to the liberation of Western Europe over their more obvious interests in the Pacific.

Attlee's remark also echoed a more long-standing vision which the British have had of their relationship to Western Europe and the rest of the world. Since the sixteenth century, they have seen themselves as a maritime power whose occasional involvement in the politics of continental Europe had always been more trouble than it was worth. In one of the *Yes, Minister* programmes broadcast on BBC television in the early 1980s, 'The Writing on the Wall', the career civil servant, Sir Humphrey Appleby, explains to his Minister, Jim Hacker, that the British government has

> had the same foreign policy objective for at least the last five hundred years – to create a disunited Europe. In that cause we have fought with the Dutch against the Spanish, with the Germans against the French, with the French and the Italians against the Germans, and with the French against the Italians and the Germans

and his remark, although apparently flippant, was based on a series of real historical events. In 1585, England had intervened to support the revolt of the Spanish Netherlands against Philip II of Spain, and in the War of The Spanish Succession (1702–1773) had led an alliance against France which included Austria and the Netherlands. Between 1793 and 1814, in the wars against the French Republic and the Empire of Napoleon I, Great Britain had allied herself with Austria and Prussia, as well as with Russia, to prevent Western Europe being dominated by France. Between 1914 and 1918, Great Britain was in alliance with France and Russia against Germany, with Italy being on the allied side in the first world war and that of the Axis in the second. During the Cold War (1946–1989), Britain was in alliance with France, Germany and Italy against the Soviet Union, the Russian power which then threatened to dominate Europe.

The English also coupled what was basically a policy of *Realpolitik*, in which the balance of power in Europe was maintained by enabling their potential enemies to cancel one another out, with a moral vision of their relationship with Europe which was perhaps less securely based. In their view, each of the régimes against which British armed forces had intervened on the Continent was characterised by a peculiarly unpleasant way of treating its own subjects and of behaving towards its neighbours. For the English, the Spain of Philip II was a proselytising, Catholic power which had expelled its own Jewish population in 1492 and seemed bent on persecuting heretics wherever they could be found. In what English historians themselves call the Whig theory of history, Louis XIV had shown a similar indifference to the rights of minorities and to the idea of religious freedom when he had decided, in 1685, to expel a million or so Protestants from France. Like Philip II, he had also looked to the English like a man bent on dominating Western Europe from a military as well as an ideological point of view, and the dictatorship which Napoleon I established in 1799 seemed to the English – and, perhaps, to others – to be pursuing precisely the same objective. The principal aim of German policy during the first world war was to reduce France to satellite status; in the second, to murder as many Jews as possible while imposing a permanent dictatorship over everyone else.[3]

There was, it is true, more than a touch of self-righteousness about the way in which the English looked at their history. It also showed a marked tendency to neglect the way in which they too had persecuted heretics, conquered Wales, massacred the Irish and the Scots, and imposed legal penalties on Roman Catholics which did not even begin to disappear until the Catholic Emancipation Act of 1829. But the behaviour of nation states is very frequently governed by a vision of themselves which lacks a firm basis in objective reality, and the British governments in the 1940s and 1950s were also influenced in their attitude to the ECSC by a number of other, more tangible political and economic factors.

On 1 January 1948 all the coal mines in Great Britain had passed into public ownership, and in 1949 the Labour Party, which since 1945 had had a majority of over a hundred in the House of Commons, had nationalised the steel industry as well. The ECSC was based on a mixture of private and public ownership. The coal mines had been nationalised in France, but not in Germany. In neither country had the steel industry been nationalised, and the speed with which the German free enterprise economy was recovering from the destruction of the second world war suggested that there would be little chance of the Federal Republic embarking on the socialism which the then majority party in the United Kingdom considered essential for a healthy economy.

The High Authority for the ECSC consisted of representatives of the six member states. Their decisions were subject to inspection and discussion by a Parliamentary Assembly consisting of members chosen from among deputies elected to the national parliaments in Belgium, France, Italy, Luxembourg, the Netherlands and West Germany, and an independent court was established to be responsible for interpreting the treaty whose signature in Paris on 18 April 1951 had brought the six countries together. But neither the High Authority itself, nor the embryo of what was to become the European Parliament, directed the utilisation of resources in the way that a national government did at the time when dealing with its own nationalised industries. The Authority fixed quotas, offered guaranteed prices and set out rules for free and equal competition. It then let the market do the rest, an idea which was anathema to the philosophy of the party which then held power in Great Britain.

The British reluctance to involve themselves in the process of European unification was also reinforced by a series of events which began outside Europe and echoed tensions already developing between the Soviet Union and its Western allies in their struggle against Nazi Germany. Even before 1945, the Soviet Union had shown that it had no intention of allowing

Western-style, parliamentary governments to be established in the countries which, like Poland, had been liberated from the Germans only to be occupied by the Red Army. The USSR established satellite governments in Albania, Bulgaria and Hungary, and on 25 February 1948, destroyed the semi-independent government of Czechoslovakia by inspiring a *coup d'état* whose brutality can be judged by the fact that the Prime Minister, Jan Mazaryk, was thrown out of a window and killed.

On its defeat in 1945, Germany had been divided into four zones, each to be occupied by one of the victorious powers of Great Britain, France, the United States and the USSR. The Soviet government treated its zone, officially transformed in October 1949 into the German Democratic Republic, in the same way as it treated the other countries it had occupied in 1944 and 1945, imposing a one-party system on the same model as the one which had existed in Russia itself since the revolution of 1917. Seen from the West, the object of what Winston Churchill was to call at Fulton, Missouri on 5 March 1946 the 'Iron Curtain' which had 'descended across the continent from Stettin in the Baltic to Trieste in the Adriatic' seemed to be to shelter a collection of régimes which were preparing an attack on Western Europe under the leadership of the Soviet Union.

The sudden invasion, on Saturday, 24 June 1950, of South Korea by well-armed forces from the Communist north consequently looked at the time very like one of the probes by which Hitler had successfully proved in the 1930s that the capacity of parliamentary democracies to resist military aggression was strictly limited. Hitler also liked to carry out his surprise moves at the weekend, when normal people's minds were on more enjoyable matters, and the fact that Saturday, 24 June 1950 was only two days before the beginning of the Wimbledon tennis tournament added insult to injury. It was on Saturday, 7 March 1936, that Hitler had invaded the demilitarised zone of the Rineland, and on Sunday, 13 March 1938 that he had succeeded in breaking another article of the Versailles Treaty by reuniting Germany and Austria by what was known as the *Anschluss*, or merging.[4] In September 1938, he had bullied the British and French into breaking their alliance with Czechoslovakia and agreeing to the transfer to Germany of the Sudetenland. He had then broken the Munich agreements by taking over what remained of Czechoslovakia on 15 March 1939 – for once, a Wednesday.

The United Kingdom, the United States and France had already received a comparable warning shot across the bows from Stalin's USSR in June 1948, when the Soviet authorities blocked all the land and canal routes to West Berlin. Like Germany itself, Berlin had been partitioned in 1945 into four occupied zones, but it had the disadvantage, for the Western allies, of lying ninety miles inside the Russian occupied zone. The attempt to use this land blockade to force France, Great Britain and the United States to withdraw their forces from West Berlin did not succeed. Between 24 June 1948 and 12 May 1949, American, British and French aircraft flew a total of 200,000 flights to furnish Berlin with the supplies which the 2,500,000 inhabitants of West Berlin needed to keep alive.

Although this included a substantial amount of coal to enable the Berliners to survive a particularly harsh winter, it also meant that more supplies of coke and coal were available for the rapidly growing industry of West Germany, an incidental example of the way in which the Cold War contributed to the revived prosperity of Western Europe after 1945. But the Berlin blockade also pointed to the existence of an Eastern bloc whose foreign policy was sufficiently aggressive to create what was felt as an urgent need for the West to rearm. The invasion of South Korea on 24 June 1950 consequently seemed like another of the incidents which meant that the course of European unification, begun with the signature of the Treaty of Paris in April 1951, could be successful only if it coincided with a general programme of European rearmament, accompanied by a movement towards military as well as economic and political unification.

This vision of a common European defence policy inspired and organised by the Europeans themselves nevertheless failed to translate itself into reality. The military measures taken to protect Western Europe against any incursion from the East may have been fully justified and certainly provided a shield behind which the process of European unification was able to take place. However, they have remained largely separate from the moves towards a united Europe which had begun in 1951 with the establishment of the ECSC. Already, on 2 April 1949, over two years before the signature of the Treaty of Paris establishing the ECSC, the United States had made a fundamental change in its foreign policy by committing itself to a peacetime alliance which guaranteed its immediate intervention to defend another state outside North America. The twelve countries which signed the North Atlantic Treaty establishing the North Atlantic Treaty Organisation (NATO) in Paris on 2 April 1949, were Belgium, Canada, Denmark, France, Iceland, Italy, Luxembourg, the Netherlands, Norway, Portugal, the United Kingdom and the United States. They were joined in 1952 by Greece and Turkey, in 1955 by the German Federal Republic, and in 1982 by Spain.

The remark frequently made at the time was that NATO had been created to keep the Americans in, the Russians out, the Germans down and the French calm was a fairly accurate summary of its basic aims, as well as what proved to be a useful guide to its long-term achievement. For what NATO did was provide a protective framework in which the Western Europeans could do more than count on the only power then able to rival the Soviet Union in military capacity, the United States of America. It also enabled them to take part in a defence programme which avoided the deep divisions inseparable from any attempt to create a wholly unified and purely European army.

There was, indeed, a marked contrast between the successful establishment of NATO and the collapse at the end of August 1954 of the attempt to create the European Defence Community (EDC). In the case of NATO, the sovereign states of Belgium, Canada, Denmark, France, Iceland, Italy, Luxembourg, the Netherlands, Norway, Portugal, the United Kingdom and the United States signed a treaty saying that an attack on one would be an attack on all. The first Allied Supreme Commander in Europe was General Eisenhower, the symbol of continuity in American politics. In 1952, he was to be elected President of the United States as the candidate of the Republican Party, after having served President Roosevelt, a Democrat, as Commander-in-Chief of the armies which had liberated Europe in 1944 and 1945. In 1949, he was serving President Truman, another Democrat, whose resolve to resist Communist aggression was proved when he unhesitatingly ordered American troops into action in June 1950 to defend South Korea against the Russian-armed North. The armed forces of the twelve member states of NATO kept their individual identity, while serving under a united command, an arrangement which differed sharply from the proposals put forward on 27 May 1952, when the six governments of Belgium, France, the Federal Republic of Germany, Italy, Luxembourg and the Netherlands signed the treaty establishing the EDC.

According to this treaty, members of the armed services of France, Italy, the Netherlands and Belgium were to serve alongside German soldiers, and to do so in units of what was intended to be an essentially European army, rather than one consisting of contingents from separate sovereign states. However, by the time the French parliament came round to voting on the treaty, in August 1954, René Pleven, who had been in power in May 1952, was no longer in office, and his successor, Pierre Mendès France, showed no enthusiasm for the idea. The proposal to establish the EDC had been strongly supported by the Americans, but there were few French people, whatever their political opinions, who did not look with intense suspicion at the possibility of rearming a Germany whose troops had been occupying France less than ten years earlier.

On 31 August 1954, deputies of the Communist left, hostile to a treaty so obviously directed against the Soviet Union, combined with their right-wing and Gaullist colleagues in the French National Assembly to prevent the treaty signed by Pleven from being ratified. It was rejected by 319 votes to 264, and the Europeans were able to sign a new treaty enabling them to set up a force to supplement NATO only when the British agreed, by the Treaty of Brussels of 23 October 1954 establishing the Western European Union (WEU), to break with centuries of tradition and keep two brigades permanently on the continent of Europe. Only this could calm French fears of a European army dominated by the Germans, and British commentators, anxious to refute the argument that the ECSC had reduced Franco-German hostility, talked instead about the Cold War with Russia, which then seemed in imminent danger of changing from ice to fire overnight, and justified their refusal to see anything new in moves towards a united Europe by quoting a stanza from Lewis Carroll's *The Hunting of the Snark*

The valley grew narrow, and narrower still,
And the evening grew darker and colder.
Till, merely from nervousness, not from good will,
They marched along, shoulder to shoulder.

MARKETS, THE COLD WAR AND ENLARGEMENT

By the mid-1950s, however, the countries of Western Europe were realising that they could manage quite well without British involvement. At the Messina conference of June 1955, which took place immediately after West Germany had recovered full sovereignty over her affairs and become a member of NATO, plans were drawn up to move from the ECSC to the creation of a European Economic Community. The treaty establishing the European Economic Community (EEC), and the European Atomic Energy Community (Euratom) was signed in Rome on 25 March 1955, with the principal aim of the larger of these two organisations being well defined by the three words in its title. It was European, in that it set out to deepen and develop the achievements of the ECSC, and separated itself economically from the rest of the world by a Common External Tariff.

All goods, from whatever source, paid the same rate of duty, whatever the country from which they originated, or into which they first entered. In the administrative language Brussels developed they are known as 'Third Countries', a term which sounds slightly odd in English, being a direct transliteration of the French 'pays tiers'. In English it also has the disadvantage of evoking – quite incorrectly – what used to be called Third World or under-developed countries. This is not the case. A 'Third Country' is merely a country which is not a member of the European Union, and is thus a category which includes countries as different from one another as Tibet and Uruguay, Japan and Uganda, and the United States of America and the People's Republic of China, but which all have one feature in common, they are not European.

In its insistence on industry and commerce, and not on political and military matters, the Community was also economic. But it was, in the view of its creators, a Community, rather than simply a common market. While each state retained its individuality, and sought to work harmoniously with its partners, it felt linked with them by other considerations apart from those of financial and material self-interest. In addition to the aim of creating closer economic co-operation, and a more rapid increase in the standard of living, article 2 of the Treaty of Rome spoke of establishing closer relationships between the states brought together under the treaty.

In the case of Euratom, the aim was the more immediate one of developing the means whereby Western Europe might become less dependent upon oil imports from America and the Middle East. Already, in the autumn of 1956, Western Europeans had been sharply reminded by the Suez Crisis of October–November of that year of how easily their economy could be disrupted by a sudden interruption in the supply of oil from the Middle East, and the details given of this crisis in the Chronology are also a reminder of the problems which could arise in the relationship between Great Britain and France and the United States of America.

Although the term 'common market' does not occur in the official title of the Treaty of Rome, article 8 speaks of how 'a common market' will be gradually established over a transitional period of twelve years, and article 38 states that 'the common market extends to agriculture and trade in agricultural products'. One of the principal methods for achieving these aims is given as the establishment of a common external trade policy as well as common agricultural and fisheries policies. Article 3 of the Treaty of Rome also speaks of the need to co-ordinate economic policies, to harmonise social policies, to create a common transport policy, and to establish a social fund capable of improving working conditions throughout the Community.

Between July and November 1957, the Treaty of Rome was ratified by the parliaments of Belgium, France, the Federal Republic of Germany, Italy, Luxembourg and the Netherlands, and it came into effect on 1 January 1958. Its long-term aim may well have been to unify Europe politically, and commentators in the United Kingdom who are suspicious of continental Europeans in general, and of Germans in particular, frequently quote the remark which Dr Walter Hallstein, the first President of the European Commission, made in 1961 'We are not in business at all. We are in politics'. The European Community, especially in its early years, nevertheless followed the example of the 1951 Treaty of Paris, setting up the ECSC, in not trying to bring about this unity at a single stroke. One of its first aims was the disappearance of all tariff barriers, and quota restrictions between the six member countries. This, it was agreed, would take place in stages over a twelve-year period. In fact, the process went so smoothly that the last customs duties between the six member states were abolished on 1 July 1968, a year and a half earlier than planned.

The free movement of manufactured goods by commercial firms was thus realised in 1968, eighteen months in advance of the original deadline set out in the Treaty of Rome in 1957, and the success of the European Community in this and other areas had a considerable impact both on its own members and on those states which, like the United Kingdom, had decided not to join. Initially, the reluctance of the United Kingdom to see any serious movement towards European unification took the form of the establishment, on 4 January 1960, of a rival organisation called the European Free Trade Organisation (EFTA), in which it grouped itself with Austria, Denmark, Norway, Portugal and Switzerland. This differed from the EEC by being primarily a free trade area, with none of the organisational structures which were so prominent a feature of the EEC, and with each country imposing separate rates of duty on goods coming from elsewhere. It also differed even more markedly from the EEC by not including agriculture.

Apart from its ability to inspire remarks about Europe being all at sixes and sevens, the creation of EFTA produced little by way of tangible results. The growth rates of its various members compared unfavourably with those of the six countries which had signed the Treaty of Rome, especially since there were few common frontiers to foster the cross-border trade which could take place so easily between France and Italy or between Germany and the Netherlands. The British expectation that the growth rate of the United Kingdom would be encouraged by increased trade with the Commonwealth was not fulfilled, partly because countries such as Australia were turning increasingly to the United States or to the new economies of the Pacific Rim, but more particularly because the growth rate of the Commonwealth countries was not very high by international standards. The most obvious sign of the relative failure of EFTA was the announcement on 10 August 1961 that the British government and Denmark were both going to apply for membership of the EEC.

This application led to the first major crisis in the development of the EEC, when General de Gaulle announced in a press conference on 14 January 1963, that Great Britain, 'a country with a maritime and insular destiny' was not ready to become a member of the EEC, and that France would therefore veto her application for membership. This announcement did not come altogether as a surprise. The negotiations for Great Britain's entry had proved quite difficult, mainly because of the basic difference between the traditional British reliance on cheap imported food and the EEC's policy of keeping food prices high enough to enable European farmers to live directly off the sale of their produce. This difference is discussed in more detail in Chapter 4, as is the nature of the disagreement which was once again to set France at odds with her partners in 1965. Then, it was an argument about the relationship between the Community and its member states, and a conflict between those who, like the French, looked for what they called 'l'Europe des Patries', and those who had a vision of a Europe in which the Community itself would gradually bring about a higher degree of political unification.

In the case of the French veto on the entry of Great Britain, it was not only a matter of a traditional rivalry between two countries which had been great powers, but which were now slipping to the middle rank, coupled with unfortunate memories of the second world war. It also involved a suspicion of the increasingly dominant role which America was playing in world politics, and a misreading of the military and political conditions in which the EEC was being allowed to develop. For in the way that the Americans saw matters, and their view was very much shared by the British, it was only the power and determination of America which was preventing the whole of Europe from being dominated by the Soviet Union.

From the moment that the Soviet Union had successfully launched the first artificial satellite, the sputnik, on 4 October 1957, its new leader, Nikita Krushchev, had adopted a foreign policy which was highly aggressive and frequently terrifying. In particular, from 28 November 1958 onwards, the Soviet Union had made a series of attempts to succeed in the policy which had inspired the blockade of West Berlin in 1948 and 1949 and then been thwarted by the airlift. Although this policy now took the apparently innocuous form of a proposal to sign a peace treaty with the German Democratic Republic, the régime more commonly known as East Germany, few observers had any illusions about what this meant. None of the member countries of NATO, of which the Federal Republic of Germany had become a member in 1955, recognised the German Democratic Republic as the legitimate government of what they still saw as the Soviet-occupied zone, and since the six member states of the EEC also belonged to NATO, this was also true of them. They consequently agreed with the United States in insisting that the Soviet Union itself remain responsible for the access routes to West Berlin, where the right of its 2,500,000 inhabitants to lead the kind of life which they chose was guaranteed by the presence of 10,000 American, French and British servicemen.

In 1939, Winston Churchill had followed up his remark about Russia being a riddle wrapped in a mystery inside an enigma by the comment that 'perhaps there is a key', and in the case of the Berlin crises of the late 1950s and early 1960s, it is a key which is not all that difficult to find. The threat to sign a peace treaty with the German Democratic Republic was less innocent than it seemed, and there were a number of occasions when Mr Krushchev was not reluctant to spell out what it meant. The launching of the sputnik, he declared, was a sign that Russia was now at least America's equal in modern technological warfare, if not her superior. It could therefore be quite dangerous for the United States of America to insist on maintaining access rights to West Berlin, since any attempt to send convoys through to that city, if they refused to allow their documents to be checked by the East German authorities, would inevitably meet the resistance which the Soviet Union was clearly in a position to offer one of her allies whose new sovereignty was being so obviously defied.

Better by far, insisted Mr Krushchev, to accept that the German Democratic Republic was now a fully sovereign state, with the obvious corollary that the division of Germany was permanent only in so far as it was now West Germany which should give up all hopes of unification. Indeed, and this was clearly the Soviet aim in also insisting that West Berlin be transformed into a 'Free City' in which no foreign troops would be garrisoned, it would be far better to accept that Germany should then follow the example of Berlin and become neutral in the contest between socialism and capitalism which, Mr Krushchev frequently remarked, was doomed by the force of history to end with the triumph of the former.

Had the West given way on Berlin, it is highly unlikely that the EEC would have developed in the way it did. From its beginnings in the ECSC of 1951, it had been fuelled by the increasingly dynamic economy of West Germany, and any withdrawal of this dynamism would have almost certainly led to its collapse. But it is extremely unlikely that a Germany which had accepted to cut its ties with the United States and its other allies, and adopted the neutrality demanded by the Soviet Union, would have been able to remain a member. It was not until after the ending of the Cold War between 1989 and 1991 that Austria, a neutral country since 1955, had been able to join, and it has always been a defining condition for membership of the EEC that states should be parliamentary democracies on the Western model. It is improbable that this would have remained the case for a neutralised West Germany which the United States had shown itself so visibly unable to protect. It would, it is true, have ceased to be what the Soviet Union said it was, a *revanchard* power seeking to reverse the result of the second world war. But it would also have very clearly swung into the political orbit dominated by the Soviet Union.

Between the Soviet note of 28 November 1958 insisting that the United States, France and the United Kingdom withdraw their troops from West Berlin and the Cuban missile crisis of late October 1962, international politics was dominated by the future of West Berlin. Tension was particularly high in Europe in the summer of 1961, with the building from Sunday, 13 August onwards of the wall separating East from West Berlin, but it reached its peak on the other side of the world during the Cuban missile crisis on 22–28 October 1962.

This became public on 22 October, when President Kennedy announced that there was strong evidence to show that the Soviet Union had broken its promise not to put nuclear weapons on Cuba, and was rapidly installing medium-range nuclear missiles there. After the United States had shown its determination to prevent this process being completed by establishing a sea blockade of Cuba, the Soviet Union finally agreed, on 26 October, to withdraw its missiles, and tension between the two superpowers lessened everywhere. This was especially the case in Western Europe, and no more was heard of the need to put an end to the right of France, Great Britain and the United States to keep their forces in West Berlin. The way was open not only to the official agreements of 1971 which gave permanent form to their presence, but also to the dramatic week in early November 1989 when the Berlin Wall came down altogether.

It had nevertheless been a close-run thing, and it is easy to imagine what could have happened if the United States surveillance planes had not noticed the missiles on Cuba, or if President Kennedy had not reacted so effectively to their presence. A discreet telephone call from Mr Krushchev would have asked President Kennedy if he really did wish to persist with his policy of defending West Berlin now that Washington and New York were in such easy range of the missiles on Cuba, and one of two things could have happened. Either the United States would have agreed to let West Berlin go, with all the consequences which this involved for Western Europe and the EEC; or the Soviet Union might have decided to try a new blockade of Berlin, pushed the United States too far, and caused an atomic war by miscalculation.

Not everyone, of course, links together the disputed status of West Berlin and the Cuban missile crisis in quite this way, and de Gaulle's veto on British entry into the EEC in January 1963 suggests that he in particular had a different reading of the situation. For him, as he later made clear by his withdrawal of French troops from the combined NATO command structure and in other actions mentioned in the Chronology, the danger to Europe lay not in the ambitions of the Soviet Union but in the desire of the Americans to exercise in Europe the same kind of commercial and cultural imperialism which he saw them as already practising in Central and South America.

It was not that de Gaulle was prepared to compromise on the question of Berlin. Unlike Mr Macmillan, whose visit to Moscow in February 1959 seemed like the prelude to a repetition of Neville Chamberlain's surrender of the territorial integrity of Czechoslovakia in Munich in September 1938, de Gaulle showed a characteristic refusal to admit any compromise. This enabled him to show Konrad Adenauer who his most reliable friends were likely to be in any crisis, and prepared the way for the fundamental shift in French foreign policy represented by the treaty of co-operation between France and Germany which de Gaulle and Adenauer signed on 22 January

1963. But de Gaulle did see Great Britain's entry into the European Community as a kind of 'Trojan horse'. Allow the British to come in, and the domination of 'Anglo-Saxons', as de Gaulle was in the habit of calling them, would inevitably follow, and he made his attitude quite clear when he said at his press conference of 14 January 1963 that the cohesion of all the members of the EEC would not last long after Great Britain had become a member. Instead, as he put it, there would be nothing but 'a colossal Atlantic community dependent upon America, which would not take long to absorb the European Community'. This, he added, was not at all what France wanted to create, which was 'a specifically European construction', clearly in the sense of one from which the United States was excluded.[5]

De Gaulle may also have had more personal reasons for his veto. He had never liked the English, and saw them as having consistently humiliated him during the second world war when he had had to install his headquarters in London. He was also understandably reluctant to reduce French influence in Europe by letting in another country of comparable size to France, and memories of German behaviour between 1939 and 1945 were still sufficiently strong for France to be the only major country in the EEC to be able to take diplomatic initiatives. The same motives which inspired his veto in 1963 when the British application had been put forward by a Conservative government were still important enough in his eyes in November 1967, when the Labour administration of Harold Wilson applied for entry. It was not until after de Gaulle's retirement from office in 1969, and replacement by Georges Pompidou, that the negotiations which led to Great Britain's final acceptance on 1 January 1973 could get underway.

Before then, however, a further crisis set France at odds with its five co-signatories of the Treaty of Rome in 1957. Neither West Germany, Italy, Luxembourg, Belgium or the Netherlands had supported de Gaulle's veto on British application for membership, and there was a comparable lack of support for France's attitude in the crisis sparked off by the proposal, put forward in June 1965, by the first President of the European Commission, Walter Hallstein, to create a more independent Community budget. The way he suggested of doing this was to transfer more and more of the duties levied on goods entering the Community from Third Countries to a fund whose use would be decided by the central administrative bodies of the Community, thus taking an important step towards creating a central Community authority which would be independent of the separate member states.

The French objected to what they saw as an attempt to water down the sovereignty traditionally enjoyed by national governments, and expressed their disapproval by adopting the policy known as the 'empty chair'. This meant that they withdrew for seven months from all the committees and other bodies which ran the EEC, so that no further progress could be made.

Only in January 1966 was the problem solved, and even then on what has proved to be a fairly contentious basis. By what was known as the 'Luxembourg compromise', a member state was allowed to veto any proposition which it judged to be opposed to its 'national interests', and in the sense that this compromise marked a victory for 'l'Europe des Patries' favoured by the French over the more federalist concepts preferred by the Belgians or the Germans, de Gaulle can be said to have gained as clear a victory as he had already done in his 1963 veto of the British application for membership, and was to win again in 1967.

De Gaulle's withdrawal from politics in April 1969 led to a change in French policy, and thus to what might be seen as the third chapter in the process which led from the establishment of the ECSC in 1951 to the Maastricht Treaty of 1991 and the creation of the European Union. From 1951 to 1957, the six states which had signed the 1951 Treaty of Paris were learning to co-operate on economic matters, and the signature of the Treaty of Rome in 1957 showed how well they had succeeded. In retrospect, it now seems fortunate that the project to establish a European Defence Community came to nothing. Its failure made the Europeans realise how important it was to maintain progress on the economic front, and it could be argued that traditional alliances of the type represented by NATO offer a better way of defending oneself than an army in which units from different nations are merged together. However, the process of enlargement which began in 1973 brought new problems with it, as well as new opportunities.

When, on 1 January 1973, the United Kingdom, Denmark and Ireland became members of the Community, they were allowed a five-year transitional period in which to integrate their economies into those of the countries already in the European Community. However, in a way which differentiated the 1970s and 1980s from the period in which the first six member states began the process of European integration, this first enlargement was overshadowed in a very negative way by the consequences of events outside Europe.

The twenty-two years separating the establishment of the ECSC in 1951 from the entry of Great Britain, Denmark and Ireland in 1973 had not been without their moments of international tension. But crises such as the Korean War of 1950–1953, the Soviet repression of the movement for Hungarian independence in October 1956 – the Soviet troops moved into Budapest on a Sunday – and that of Czechoslovakia in 1968, had all helped, in a way, to create the economic prosperity which later led a French economist, Jean Fourastié, to dub the period immediately following the ending of the second world war in 1945 'les trente glorieuses': the thirty glorious years. The same was true of the Berlin crises of 1958–1959 and 1961, and the Cuban missiles crisis of October 1962, and it may not have been entirely an accident that the various forms of euphoria which characterised the 1960s followed the successful conclusion of the most dangerous crisis of the Cold War.

The Cold War also made an economic contribution to the success of the movement towards European unification which had begun in April 1951 with the signature of the Treaty of Paris establishing the ECSC. By requiring the United States and its NATO allies to inject money into the economy by a process of constant rearmament, the Cold War had done precisely what Keynes had recommended as a means of putting an end to the slump of the 1930s. In his view, capitalist economies had a permanent tendency to generate insufficient demand. The only way to deal with this problem was for governments to make up for the shortfall by pumping money into the economy. This is precisely what the rearmament programmes of the Cold War did, giving rise to the paradoxical result of strengthening the capitalist economies which the Marxist theories officially inspiring the Soviet Union claimed were doomed to collapse. Had the USSR pursued a less aggressive foreign policy, it might well have allowed the capitalist world to collapse through its own inner contradictions. By continuing to behave as it did when it followed the imposition of its version of socialism on the countries occupied by the Red Army after 1945 by its various threats against West Berlin, it made an invaluable contribution to the victory of the West in the Cold War.

The crises of the 1970s and 1980s were of a different kind from those of the 1950s and 1960s. Unlike the controlled spending on armaments during the 1945–1970 period, they gave rise to a runaway inflation which seemed to threaten the survival of capitalism in just as deadly a way as the depression sparked off by the Wall Street Crash of 1929. They consequently offered more of a threat than the Cold War had ever done to the process of European integration which had begun in 1951, especially since the Community itself seemed at times to be in danger of running into the sands.

The first of these crises began on 15 August 1971, when President Nixon suspended the convertibility of the dollar. This meant the end of the system whereby all countries could buy as many dollars as they liked in order to keep part of their holdings in a currency whose value was guaranteed by the United States government. It led to the disappearance of fixed exchange rates, and to an instability which affected the exchange value of all world currencies. It thus exacerbated the problems which were already threatening the operation of the Common Agricultural Policy (CAP), and which had first shown themselves in an acute form on 10 August 1969, when the French government suddenly devalued the franc by 6.6 per cent, and the Italian government allowed the value of the lira to fall by a comparable extent.

A similar crisis was to occur in May 1971, when the Deutschmark and

Dutch guilder increased rapidly in value in comparison with the other European currencies, and the effect of both currency changes was the same. Like the devaluations carried out by the Latin and Mediterranean members of the Community, the increase in purchasing power of the guilder and the Deutschmark meant that French and Italian agricultural products suddenly became much cheaper outside France and Italy than food grown in Germany or Holland. A complicated system of Monetary Compensation Units had to be established to maintain equal competition in the market for agricultural products, and this seemed at times almost like the return of custom duties. The French and Italians had to pay an export tax to bring their agricultural products up to the same price as the food grown in the northern European, Germanic countries whose currency had not fallen in value, while the Germans and Dutch imposed what was in effect an import levy on French and Italian produce.

In the long-term, however, the monetary instability already endemic as a result of the constantly better performance of the German or Dutch economies, and made worse by President Nixon's decision also to impose a tax on imports into the United States, turned out to be what supporters of European economic integration could not help but see as a good thing. It provided a stimulus for the member countries of the European Community to try to develop a system whereby their currencies varied against one another only within defined limits, and thus encouraged moves towards economic and monetary union and the development of a European Single Currency.

The end of an international financial system based upon a stable dollar also marked the end of the period of sustained economic growth which had existed since 1945. Not only did it encourage the inflation which became one of the great threats to world prosperity in the 1970s. It also gave rise to the rather subversive view that the increased prosperity which the six original members of the European Community had enjoyed throughout the 1950s and 1960s would have happened anyway, whether they had chosen to form a customs union or not. The rising tide which raises all boats could well have been the product of a general international prosperity which had, from time to time, enabled even the British economy to show signs of working satisfactorily. For while it is true, as Pierre Gerbert points out in *La Construction de l'Europe*, that trade within the EEC increased between 1958 and 1970, by a factor of six, and trade between the EEC and the rest of the world by more than 70 per cent,[6] comparable increases were visible elsewhere, especially in North America and the economies of the Pacific Rim.

There was also another event which made the entry of the United Kingdom into the European Community in January 1973 seem initially like the kiss of death for its fellow members, a warning that the prosperity marking the first fifteen years of the Community's existence was at an end. This event was the decision of the Organisation of Petroleum Exporting Countries (OPEC), in the autumn of 1973, to quadruple the price of oil. In 1950, this would have been inconvenient for motorists, but not the body blow to the economy which it almost proved in 1973. In 1950, 75 per cent of the energy needs of Western Europe were met by coal, but by 1970, this had fallen to 20 per cent. All the economies of the industrialised world had allowed themselves to become heavily dependent upon cheap oil in a similar way, letting their coal mines run down, and refraining, for ecological reasons, from developing nuclear energy. In spite of the presence of Euratom, the success of the CAP had not been accompanied by the development of a common energy policy. The United Kingdom made it clear as soon as oil was discovered beneath the North Sea in the mid-1970s, which the increase in the world price of energy now made it worthwhile to develop, that it was for national and not general, Community use.

The oil crisis also emphasised the absence of a common foreign policy. The German Federal Republic, like Holland, tended to see the sudden increase in the price of oil as a new weapon used by the Arab states in what was then the constant aim of their foreign policy: that of destroying Israel and repeating the effects of Hitler's holocaust by driving all the Jews into the Mediterranean. Defeated on the field of battle in 1948 and 1967, and held to a draw in the fighting which began with the attack on Israel on the eve of Yom Kippour, on 6 October 1973, the Moslem states allied against Israel turned to economic warfare. To begin with, they threatened to impose a total boycott of the sale of oil on all states supporting or selling arms to Israel. They then introduced selective price rises directed against pro-Israeli states, before making the price rises general. France, which had stopped supporting Israel in 1967, and which had to import 98 per cent of its oil, took a pro-Arab line. This did not enable the French to buy oil any cheaper, and underlined the inability of the European Community to adopt a common foreign and economic policy to deal with the most serious economic crisis to affect Europe since 1945.

But the Community did not break up. Indeed, it continued to remain attractive to other countries, and its enlargement to include Greece in 1981, and Spain and Portugal in 1986, gave it a more Mediterranean flavour which redressed the imbalance created by the entry of Denmark, Ireland and the United Kingdom in 1973. The first expansion of the European Community had made it look like a grouping dominated by countries in northern Europe whose culture was either basically Protestant, like that of Holland, or officially secular like that of France, or a mixture of Catholic and Protestant as in the case of Germany. The admission of Spain and Portugal maintained the Latin and Catholic identity which had been there with the presence from the very beginning with Italy, as well as of a France which still occasionally saw itself as 'la fille aînée de l'Église' (the eldest daughter of the Church), and whose religious connotations found an echo in Frenchmen such as Robert Schuman and his German Catholic counterpart, Konrad Adenauer.

The enlargement of 1986 was not without its problems, though not on the scale which had immediately followed the admission of the United Kingdom in 1973. The French, in particular, were unenthusiastic about the admission of countries which were able to produce fruit and vegetables which ripened a month early south of the Pyrenees, and which thus offered serious competition to farmers in the South of France. The British were equally unenthusiastic about giving the Spanish fishing fleet access to Community waters. By 1985, the year before Spain's entry into the Community, the tonnage of this fleet was 70 per cent of that of the nine existing members put together, and disputes between the United Kingdom and Spain over fishing quotas have, as is further discussed in Chapter 4, since proved a major source of disagreement in the Community.

Neither did the United Kingdom feel enthusiastic about the possibility of seeing its contributions to the Community budget used to enable the Spanish and Portuguese economies to develop to the point where they too, like those of France and West Germany, could become serious and successful rivals to British industry. The British had pressed heavily in the negotiations leading up to the entry of the United Kingdom into the Community on 1 January 1973 for the creation of a regional development fund. Since British farming was already more efficient than that of any of the existing member countries apart from Holland, the United Kingdom was clearly not going to benefit very much from the funds available under the Agricultural Guidance and Guarantee Fund whose aims and workings are discussed in Chapter 4.

This fund was aimed at enabling the relatively inefficient and over-manned agricultural systems of France and Italy to bring themselves up to the point where they could charge lower prices for their products, and it was clear from the beginning that the United Kingdom was going to lose from the system whereby member states paid 90 per cent of the duties levied on agricultural products under the Common External Tariff and entrusted to the Community's 'own resources' fund administered by the Commission in Brussels, while retaining only 10 per cent for collection costs. Since the British were hoping to recoup their losses under the CAP by grants from a regional development fund which would provide help for depressed areas such as the North East, Liverpool and Northern Ireland, they were again not over-enthusiastic at the idea of poorer countries such as Spain or Portugal competing for money from the Regional Development Fund established in 1975.

The admission of Spain and Portugal, which were having considerable problems in developing a modern economy and democratic political structures, was nevertheless finally achieved, though after a delay which was not explicable, as had been that imposed on Great Britain in 1963 and 1967, by a combination of traditional rivalry, personal spite, and a misreading of the very different aims and objectives pursued by the Soviet Union and the United States of America. Spain had already applied for permission in 1962, but had been turned down on the grounds that the régime imposed by General Franco after his victory in the civil war of 1936–1939 was undemocratic, and showed no sign of changing.

After the death of Franco in 1975, Spain had reapplied in 1979, together with Portugal, and the seven-year wait offers an instructive contrast with the speed with which Austria, Finland and Sweden were accepted as members in the 1990s. These three countries all had well-developed economies which increased the purchasing power of the inhabitants of what had, by then, become the European Union, and a good record in human rights. Spain and Portugal, in contrast, were poor countries whose lack of a strong democratic tradition reflected the way in which they had, since the eighteenth century, remained isolated from the intellectual and cultural developments which had brought about the modernisation of Western Europe.

Neither of the two Iberian cultures had been touched by the Reformation of the sixteenth century, or by the Enlightenment of the eighteenth, and their separation from the political changes brought about by the Age of Reason was a major factor in making them so vulnerable to the right-wing totalitarianism of the 1919–1939 period.[7] The process of European unification begun in 1950 by the Schuman proposal was very much in the tradition of the eighteenth century Enlightenment, with its insistence on the importance of applied science, of intellectual tolerance and on the contract theory of government exemplified by the English revolution of 1688. Until the death of Franco put an end to the dictatorship which he had imposed on Spain since his victory in the Spanish civil war in April 1939, and the events of 1975 overthrew the authoritarian régime imposed in Portugal in 1932 by Oliveira Salazar, neither country fulfilled the political criteria required for membership of the EEC.

The entry of Spain and Portugal suggests a reply to the view that the Community has no right to call itself European since it does not include such indisputably European states as Hungary, Poland, Romania, the Czech Republic and the Slovak Republic. Until the late 1980s, when the Russians withdrew their army of occupation and allowed each satellite country to go its own way, such states were one-party dictatorships, as intolerant of dissent as Franco's Spain, Salazar's Portugal or the Greece of the colonels had been until they were overthrown in 1974. As the countries of Eastern Europe become more democratic, they too are becoming eligible for membership, even though they will, like Greece and Portugal, bring relatively little to the Community by way of economic gain.

The French and Germans, and even occasionally the English, nevertheless see the money which it costs to have countries such as Spain, Portugal and Greece as well spent, and may well take the same attitude towards the Czech Republic and Hungary. The further the democracies of Western Europe can extend their political influence, as well as their economic system, the safer they will feel; and it may well be, now that the Russians have decided to withdraw their troops and allow the countries of Eastern Europe to develop their own economic and political systems, that the ex-satellites of the Soviet Union will achieve, if not full membership of the Community, at least a closer association.

This would be fully in keeping with the original, primarily political aims of the founding fathers of the ECSC. Their original intention was the political one of avoiding another war between France and Germany. In the 1990s, one of the main political aims of the European Community is to ensure that the states of Eastern Europe develop a viable form of parliamentary democracy as a permanent replacement for the Communist totalitarianism from which they have just escaped.

An additional political aim inspiring the creation of the first European Community, in 1958, was to build a Europe sufficiently prosperous and united to be able to stand up by itself, eventually without American help, to what was then seen as the very aggressive foreign policy of the Soviet Union. To allow the former satellites of the USSR to join would, in this respect, be the Community's own contribution to the final winning of the Cold War. Russian Marxism, having failed to maintain its hold over Poland, the Czech Republic, the Slovak Republic and Hungary, is being required to allow these four countries to accompany the former East Germany in rejoining the Europe to which they have traditionally belonged, and Russia itself seems anxious to follow the same path.

2 Organisation and powers

INITIATIVES, DECISIONS AND VOTES

The Commission

There were a number of reasons why the United Kingdom refused to join the European Coal and Steel Community (ECSC) in 1951, and why it also declined the invitation to be a founder member of the European Community in 1958. One of these, already mentioned in Chapter 1, was the refusal of the Labour government of 1945 to involve itself in an organisation which was seen as based on the essentially capitalist principle of private ownership as the means of production, distribution and exchange. Another, which is discussed in Chapter 4, was an awareness of the incompatibility between the traditional way British agriculture was organised and the ambitions inspiring the Common Agricultural Policy (CAP) set up by the 1957 Treaty of Rome.

A third, which remains linked to the hostility towards continental Europeans inspiring movements such as Sir James Goldsmith's Referendum Party and books like Bernard Connolly's *The Rotten Heart of Europe* (1995),[1] was the fear of a loss of national independence, linked with the view that any unified Europe to emerge from the process begun by the Treaty of Paris would be one governed by an unelected bureaucracy. It was Clement Attlee who introduced what was to remain a constant factor in criticism in the United Kingdom of the form which European unification has so far taken when he said in a debate on the Schuman plan in the House of Commons in 1950, that

> We on this side are not prepared to accept the principle that the most vital economic forces of this country should be handed over to an authority which is utterly undemocratic and responsible to nobody.[2]

Whether justified or not, this fear reflected an awareness of the unusual nature of institutions established by the 1957 Treaty of Rome, and which are significantly different from those adopted by any other international organisation. Unlike the United Nations Organisation (UN), or a military alliance such as the North Atlantic Treaty Organisation (NATO), the European Union is a body to which member states give up a certain number of their traditional, sovereign rights. This was already true of the ECSC of 1951, by which the six member states gave up the power to decide the detailed way in which two of their major industries would be run, and was even truer of the European Economic Community (EEC) of 1958.

Its six member states, the same countries which had signed the Treaty of Paris of 1951, agreed to give up any individual power to levy import duties on goods entering their territory, as well as the right to award preferential treatment to their own industries when these were in competition with those situated in another member state. They also gave up the right to limit access to the labour market to their own citizens. They did so, moreover, by accepting to work within the framework of a set of institutions whose decisions were taken collectively but which remained binding whatever objections they may have originally had to their formulation.

The European Free Trade Area (EFTA) was very much the creation of the United Kingdom. It did not include agriculture, and had a weak administrative structure, with little loss of national sovereignty. The institutions of the European Community, in contrast, are a clear indication as to how membership reduces the direct control which a member state has over its own economic affairs. In the UN, neither the Security Council nor the General Assembly has the right to take initiatives. They have to wait for an individual member state to do so.

Each of the five Permanent Members of the Security Council retains the right to block any measure by the use of the veto. If a member state does not agree with the policy decided by a majority of the other countries, it simply refuses to join in. Unless it breaks the law, as Iraq did when it invaded the territory of Kuwait in 1990, there is nothing that the UN can do about it. Although there is no means of knowing what would have happened if a war had broken out between the Soviet Union and one of the member states of NATO, these states retain a comparable freedom of political manoeuvre in peace time. When France decided in 1966 to withdraw her forces from the NATO military command structure, there was no doubt of her right as a fully sovereign state to do so.

Each of the sixteen member states of NATO has a representative on its permanent Council. These representatives must, however, follow the instructions given to them by their government. There is no way in which the Organisation can take independent decisions on its own behalf. It must wait for the states which signed the 1949 treaty to act in accordance with what they, in consultation with one another, decide what to do. In the European Union, in contrast, the initiative to act comes from the Commission, a body which exists independently of the individual states, and which alone among all the other bodies of the European Union has the right to take initiatives and introduce legislation on behalf of the Union itself. While it is open to an individual state to put forward proposals to the Council of Ministers, they do so only in their own name, and are thus vulnerable to be seen as advancing national rather than Community interests.

From 1958 to 1973 the Commission had nine members: two from France, two from Italy, two from West Germany, one from Luxembourg, one from the Netherlands and one from Belgium. Since the admission of Great Britain, Ireland and Denmark in 1973, of Greece in 1981, of Spain and Portugal in 1986 and of Finland, Austria and Sweden in 1994, its membership has risen to twenty. France, Germany, Italy, Spain and the United Kingdom each have two and Austria, Belgium, Denmark, Finland, Greece, Ireland, Luxembourg, the Netherlands, Portugal and Sweden one each.

Commissioners are appointed for a five-year, renewable term. A change introduced at the time of the Maastricht Treaty of 1991 means that the period of office of the Commission coincides with the period for which the European Parliament is elected. Commissioners are proposed for membership by the country of which they are citizens, but must be acceptable to all member states. Once appointed, Commissioners can be reappointed indefinitely, so long as they remain acceptable to all member states. An individual Commissioner can be dismissed only by the Court of Justice, acting on a proposal from the Council of Ministers. This has not so far happened.

The Commission as a whole is confirmed in office by a vote of the European Parliament. It can also be required to resign if a vote of censure is passed against it in the European Parliament, though this again has not yet happened. The Parliament must also be consulted before the President of the Commission is appointed. This appointment, like that of the Commission itself, is by a unanimous vote of the member countries. The longest serving President of the Commission is Jacques Delors, who held office from 1985 to 1994.

Once appointed, Commissioners do not represent the state of which they are citizens. They cannot accept instructions from the government of their home state, but must act in accordance with what they consider to be the best interests of the Community as a whole. Whereas the diplomats representing their countries in the United Nations General Assembly, or on the Security Council, must follow the instructions given to them by their governments, European Commissioners can, if they feel that this best serves the interests of the Community, act against what they know to be the wishes of their home government.

Like other bureaucracies in states which have elected legislative assemblies and observe the rule of law, the Commission is not a decision-making body. Its proposals have to be approved by the Council of Ministers, a body whose powers and functions are discussed on p. 30. Although the activities of the European Commission come under the scrutiny of the European Parliament and the Court of Auditors, whose powers and functions are discussed on p. 41, the European Commission is not subject to the same kind of control as the Cabinet, or Council of Ministers, in a conventional democratic régime.

There, members are individually responsible either to the Head of State, as in the Constitution of the Fifth French Republic or of the United States of America, or to an elected assembly, as members of the government are responsible to the House of Commons in the British system. Neither is there any way in which a member of the Commission, like a Cabinet minister in a parliamentary democracy, can be asked to resign by Parliament while the Cabinet as a whole carries on its work. The Commission's responsibility is that of a joint body exercising corporate leadership. It can be dismissed only as a body, and then only by a two-thirds majority in the European Parliament.

The recommendations of the Commission must be approved by the Council of Ministers and examined by the European Parliament before coming into effect, and it is there that account is taken of national as well as of sectional interests. But the right of the Commission, and of the Commission alone, to take initiatives on behalf of the European Union helps to explain why the organisation which began life as the EEC has moved so steadily forward to the stated aim of economic and political integration. It is like the engine of a car, carrying it along whatever reservations some of the passengers may occasionally have about the speed or direction, and it is in this respect that the Commission can be seen as exemplifying some of the advantages as well as the drawbacks of a bureaucratic style of government as distinct from that of a parliamentary democracy.

A democratically elected government is, by definition, only there for a limited period of time. If it loses the next election, then its plans are replaced by those of the opposition. A bureaucracy, in contrast, is always there, and its plans acquire from its very permanence a momentum denied to those of a government required to explain and justify its policies not only to the opposition but also to its own backbenchers. A bureaucracy has plenty of time to work out what it is going to do, and is not required to consult anybody else during its deliberations. If it does not conduct its deliberations in secret, it retains the freedom of choice as to whom to consult and whose views to adopt. The Commission naturally does this, since it would otherwise encounter too many obstacles. But it nevertheless retains the invaluable right of choosing the terrain on which action will be taken.

A government responsible to an elected assembly has its daily actions submitted to continual scrutiny, and has to satisfy sectional interests among its own supporters at the same time as it replies to criticisms from the press, from parliament and from the opposition. It also has to spend a certain amount of time and effort wondering about how not to lose the next election. A bureaucracy also develops a strong group identity. Its members may be anxious for promotion, but they are not jockeying for position in the way that the members of a cabinet sometimes are.

A bureaucracy also acquires an immense amount of knowledge and technical expertise. In the case of the European Commission, this enables it to exercise responsibility for managing the budget for the Common Agricultural Policy (CAP), the European Regional Development Fund, the Social Fund and the fund for Foreign Aid and for Administration. The Commission employs the largest number, 15,000, of the total of 24,500 people directly employed by the different administrative bodies of the European Union, with 3,000 of these Commission employees being translators and interpreters. It is these permanent administrators, perhaps even more than the Commissioners themselves, who are in a position to give its policies their continuity, a fact illustrated by the details accompanying the announcement on 12 February 1997, that David Williamson, the Secretary General of the European Commission, was to take early retirement at the age of 63.

Since David Williamson had already been in office for ten years, and could have carried on to the age of 65 if he had so wished, the period of time during which he was in a position to influence the development and formulation of policy was considerably longer than that of even the most successful higher civil servants in Great Britain, and far longer than that of the vast majority of elected politicians. Margaret Thatcher held office for only ten years, while the ability of François Mitterrand to remain President of France for fourteen years reflects an aspect of the Constitution of the Fifth Republic which he had denounced as thoroughly undemocratic before his own election to the Presidency in 1981.

Like all other bureaucratic organisations, the European Commission works out techniques for dealing with obstacles, understands the workings of other bureaucracies and may even exchange favours with them. It accepts into its midst only people whom it knows it will like, and who will be quick to understand how, in spite of comments from the outside, it knows best. This may sometimes well be the case, and organisations based on adoption and co-option have lasted much longer than those where power is handed down on an hereditary principle or obtained by democratic election. The British monarchy takes pride on being able to trace its first ancestors as far back as the Danish King Egbert, who ruled from 829 to 830, and no other ruling house can claim as much. Compared to the Papacy, however, which officially dates its beginning from the advent of St Peter in AD 33, it is still a fairly recent creation.

The description of the Commission as the engine or driving force of the European Union goes hand in hand with the view expressed in 1995 by one of the Official Publications of the European Communities, *The Single Market*, when it said that the single market is 'like other aspects of the European Union: if it stops advancing, it regresses'.[3] Eurosceptics are suspicious of this ambition of the Union to make its powers constantly deeper and more extensive, and point to the dangers outlined by the historian Paul Kennedy in *The Rise and the Fall of the Great Powers* (1987) of what he calls 'imperial overstretch'. Sooner or later, they argue, a bureaucracy with over-extensive ambitions will defeat itself through not knowing where to stop, just as the territorial or maritime empires of the past have done. They consequently greet with dismay rather than applause the statement in another Community publication, *The Institutions of the European Community*, that during 1994, the Commission submitted 558 propositions to the Council of Ministers, together with 272 other documents.

The headquarters of the European Commission are in the Berlaymont building in Brussels. There has been some comment on the wastage in travelling time and transmission of documents involved in having the main bodies of the Union meet in separate places, with the Commission in Brussels, the European Parliament in Strasbourg and the Secretariat for the European Union, like the Court of Justice of the European Communities, the Court of Auditors and the European Investment Bank (see p. 42) in Luxembourg. The accusation that the Commission is a 'faceless bureaucracy' is not strictly accurate, since the names of the European Commissioners are published and perfectly well known. So, too, are their salaries, and in January 1997, the first issue of *News*, the paper put out by the Referendum Party, laid considerable emphasis on the fact that each received £147,000 a year salary, £20,000 a year housing allowance, £20,000 cost of living allowance and £5,000 personal entertainment allowance.

The Council of the European Union or Council of Ministers

The pamphlet *Serving the European Union* defines the basic decision-making process by saying that the Commission proposes, the Council approves, the Parliament advises and the Court of Justice interprets. Only the Commission has the right to introduce legislation on behalf of the Union.

It does so by bringing forward proposals which it submits to the Council of Ministers, the main decision-making body of the Union, and to the European Parliament, whose role so far has been more that of a consultative body than a legislative one.

The Council is an inter-governmental body, at which each of the fifteen states in the European Union is represented by a minister from its home government. While this is, in principle, the foreign minister, the identity of the minister attending and voting at any specific meeting depends in practice on the subject under discussion. When an aspect of the CAP is being debated, the meeting is attended by the Minister for Agriculture, when transport policy the Minister for Transport.

In the normal course of events, votes are taken by a system of weighted voting in which France, Italy, Germany and the United Kingdom each have ten votes, Spain has eight, Belgium, Greece, the Netherlands and Portugal have five each, Austria and Sweden four each, Finland, Denmark and Ireland three each and Luxembourg two. Unless a state decides to exercise its veto under what is called the 'Luxembourg compromise' (see Chapter 1, p. 17), something which very rarely happens and has been made even more difficult under the provisions of the Maastricht Treaty, a proposal from the Commission is approved if it receives what is known as a 'qualified majority' of sixty-two out of the eighty-seven votes available. A proposal made by an individual state also needs sixty-two votes, together with the support of at least ten of the member states, if it is to become a Directive (for the meaning of this term see p. 38). In practice, it is the smaller states such as Belgium or Ireland which are keenest on full European integration, and the weighted voting system is intended to ensure that they are protected against any attempt by the larger states to dominate the Community.

While the Council takes the decisions governing the relations between the European Union and the outside world, it is the Commission which represents the interests of the fifteen member states in negotiations carried out with other countries and economic groupings under the auspices of what used to be called the General Agreement on Tariffs and Trade and is now officially the World Trade Organisation. The Council has to be unanimous if it wishes to take a different view from the proposals coming to it from the European Commission, or from amendments approved by the European Parliament. The Chairmanship of the Council of Ministers rotates among the member governments on a six-monthly basis in alphabetical order according to the name of the country in its own language, with the country which chairs the Council automatically assuming the chairmanship of all its subordinate committees. If and when the European Union succeeds in adopting a common foreign policy, it is assumed that the Council of Ministers will be the forum in which it is decided.

Since the prime responsibility of the Ministers who constitute the Council remains their role in the government of their home country, discussion of matters on a day-to-day basis is carried out by a group of career diplomats, one for each country and of ambassadorial status, meeting in Brussels, known as the Committee of Permanent Representatives (COREPER), and in constant touch with the Commission. This is said to ensure a balance between a Community vision and the view of the individual states, and enables a number of non-contentious matters to be settled without detailed ministerial discussion. It is this practice which enables Klaus-Dieter Borchardt to write in *The ABC of Community Law* (European Documentation, 1993) that if the COREPER

> reaches full agreement on a proposed piece of legislation, the item is entered on the Council agenda as an A item, meaning that the Council need do no more than formally record its approval without further debate.[4]

It is the presence in Brussels of the Permanent Members of COREPER which is another aspect of the European Union that leads to the accusation that it is dominated by a bureaucracy which may well be enlightened but is nevertheless unelected. It is said to be very easy for these Members, as the Whitehall expression has it, to 'go native', as indeed Ambassadors elsewhere have been known to do, and to be far more influenced by opinion in Brussels, Strasbourg or Luxembourg than by the views held by the electors in Belgium, France, Italy or the United Kingdom.

Another way of expressing this idea is to talk about the 'democratic deficit', and to argue that at least some of the debates in the Council of Ministers should take place in public. At the moment, as Timothy Bainbridge and Anthony Teasdale point out in their invaluable *Penguin Companion to the European Union*, it is 'the only legislature in the democratic world which takes its decisions largely in secret'.[5] Were it to debate more issues in public, it is argued, the citizens of the European Union would be less tempted to think that the decisions affecting their economic future and daily lives were being taken by a closed circle which they not only had no power to influence but whose detailed mode of working was kept hidden from them.

Both the Council of Ministers and the European Council, see p. 41, have to be distinguished from the Council of Europe. This was set up in 1949 in order to foster European co-operation, especially in the field of human rights. It has thirty-four members, including Cyprus, Iceland, Liechtenstein, Malta, Norway, Switzerland and Turkey, in addition to all the countries which originally belonged to the EEC, or which have since become members of the European Union. There is, however, no connection between the Council of Europe and the European Council of Ministers, and their functions are quite different.

The European Parliament

The concept of parliamentary democracy is closely linked, in France and the United States as well as in the United Kingdom, with the role of parliament as mistress of the public purse. Since the English revolution of the seventeenth century, the view has grown up that citizens of a democracy can legally be required to pay either direct or indirect taxes only if these form part of a budget approved by a parliamentary assembly which they have had the right to elect. It may well be that the party in power is one for which these taxpayers have not voted. The convention nevertheless remains that they have had the opportunity of taking part in the debate which led to the winning of the election by their opponents. They must therefore stick to the rules of the game, and agree to pay their taxes, in the same way as they would expect their opponents to do if the result of the election had been different.

The precise mechanism by which a parliamentary assembly has ultimate control over the executive by its ability to grant or refuse it the money needed to carry on the government varies from country to country. It is not the same in the United States of America as it is in the United Kingdom, and there is again a difference with what happens in France. Final agreement on the budget in the United States is obtained only after a long series of negotiations between the President and Congress, and Americans are frequently surprised at the relative ease and rapidity with which a British government with a majority in the House of Commons succeeds in having its finance bills adopted. But the principle that a budget is legal only if it has received the approval of the elected representatives of the taxpayers who will be affected by it is the same in both countries, and the phenomenon in French politics known as 'la cohabitation' is also a reflection of the idea that the only money which can be legally raised by a government is that whose quantity and mode of collection has been approved by parliament. For when, in March 1986, President François Mitterrand found himself faced with a National Assembly dominated by the right, he had no choice but to appoint as Prime Minister a right-wing politician capable of obtaining approval for his budget. Without a legally approved budget, no government in a parliamentary democracy can last more than a day.

It is by contrast with this tradition that the powers and functions of the European Parliament make it seem a very inadequate instrument for redressing the 'democratic deficit'. The budget of the Community is derived partly from contributions made by member states, and partly from what are known as its 'own resources'. By the Treaty of Luxembourg of 22 April 1970, these consist of the duty paid on agricultural and industrial products entering the countries in the Union, and 1.4 per cent of the Value Added Tax (VAT) levied by each individual state. There is no means whereby the European Parliament can exercise any control over these, and the right of initiative which the Commission enjoys in the bringing forward of legislation also extends to the budget. The rate of duty paid by imports into the Union is the result of a long process of joint decision by the Commission and Council, and the rate of VAT forms part of the national budget of each member state. The European Parliament cannot therefore control what might be thought of as the executive of the European Union – the Commission and Council – in the way that the British parliament, or the United States Congress, can exercise power over the executive by refusing to grant supply.

The control which the European Parliament has over the Union budget is therefore limited to the way the money is spent, and here again its powers are limited in a way for which there is no parallel in traditional parliamentary democracies. Expenditure on the CAP, for example, which absorbs half of the overall budget of the Union, is managed on a day-to-day basis by the Commission, and remains under the control of the Council of Ministers.[6] In 1980, one of the first actions of the first European Parliament to be directly elected by universal suffrage, in 1979, was to exercise its right to reject the budget, and it repeated its refusal in 1984. But whereas a national government defeated on a finance bill resigns, the Commission and Council of Ministers stay in office even if the budget is not approved, and the Community itself continues on the basis of a monthly budget calculated on what happened last year.

At Westminster, individual ministers are responsible to the House, and are expected – at least in theory – to resign if a serious mistake is made in their Department. Although Commissioners are expected to be there for the parliamentary debates, this does not always happen. They can, it is true, be required to answer questions concerning their particular area of responsibility, but they are not responsible to the European Parliament in the way that a Minister is responsible to the House of Commons at Westminster. The fact of having been appointed for five years gives them the right to stay there whatever happens in their particular area of responsibility, and although members of the Council of Ministers are, in general, elected politicians responsible to their home parliament, they have no comparable responsibility to the European Parliament.

The power of the European Parliament to initiate legislation is also more limited than that of the national parliaments of the member states. Although it obtained this power when the recommendations of the Patjin report on direct election were finally accepted in 1975, what this means in fact is simply the right to ask the Commission to draw up a legislative proposal. The wording of this proposal, and the timing of its submission to the Council of Ministers, remains the prerogative of the Commission, which may withdraw or modify it at any time. There is currently no equivalent to the provision either at Westminster or in the French *Chambre des Députés* for a member to introduce the equivalent of a private member's bill. The attempt in 1976 to make the Commission as a whole resign, when a group of British Conservative Members of the European Parliament (MEPs) tried to use it to criticise the Commission's failure to deal with the problem of dairy surpluses, was defeated by an overwhelming majority.

The other attempts which have been made to enable the European Parliament to fulfil what is seen as the normal function of checking and controlling the executive have so far proved equally unsuccessful. In 1973, shortly after British entry, a change was introduced whereby members of the Commission were expected to be there to attend Parliament and answer questions. However, this requirement has not developed into the equivalent at Westminster of Prime Minister's Question Time. The questions have to be submitted in advance in written form, and the sessions at which they are answered take place at night and are poorly attended. They may not deal with matters which have been approved by the Council of Ministers on the basis of agreements between member states.

These sessions also tend to be dominated by MEPs from the United Kingdom, and thus have the disadvantage of being slightly suspect to their colleagues from the Latin and Germanic countries, where parliamentary procedure is not based on the essentially adversarial tradition characteristic of Westminster. Indeed, it could be argued that some of the criticisms directed at the European Parliament stem from an unjustified expectation on the part of the British that it should serve as a forum for a clash between government and opposition which does not really exist in the European Union. Most of the legislation which it considers is fairly technical in nature, and the reservations which may be felt about it do not, however justified in certain cases, follow party lines. As is suggested by the existence of bodies such as the Economic and Social Committee, the kind of democracy established in Brussels is consultative and participatory, not adversarial.

One of the reasons inspiring de Gaulle's two vetoes on British entry was that it would be followed by a series of moves on the part of the new members to change the rules of the club to which the United Kingdom had been admitted. The widely-held expectation in Great Britain that the European Parliament both could and would fulfil the same role in government as it does in the House of Commons suggests that his fears were not altogether unjustified. It could also be argued that the criticism of the European Parliament which is a common feature of British reservations about Europe is based not only on a misreading of its role, but on something of an idealisation of what now goes on at Westminster.

As Lord Hailsham pointed out some time ago, the British Parliament at Westminster has become something of an elected dictatorship. There are, in practice, remarkably few restrictions on the ability to change the law which a Prime Minister with a majority of more than fifty seats in the House, and an efficient team of government Whips, has in the present House of Commons. She or he may have their moments of embarrassment at Question Time, but there is nevertheless little real danger of their losing power.

The Single European Act of 1986 tried to make the European Parliament less immune to the criticism that it was mainly a talking shop by strengthening its powers in relation both to the Commission and the Council of Ministers. This Act gave the Parliament the opportunity for two readings of a proposal brought forward by the Commission, and agreed in principle by the Council. It also established a procedure whereby proposals in certain fields needed to be approved by an absolute majority (at least 313 members voting in favour) before they could become law. These included treaties between the European Union and 'Third Countries', the accession of new members, citizenship and residence rights, changes in the CAP and in the use of regional funds.

The Parliament also received the right in 1986 to conduct what is called a 'co-decision procedure' whereby it collaborates with the Council in reaching a compromise if it does not initially vote in favour of a proposal coming to it from the Commission. This procedure provides for a con-ciliation committee, made up of an equal number of representatives from the Parliament, the Council and the Commission, to look at the proposal in dispute with a view to bringing it forward in a modified form on which everyone agrees. Should no agreement be forthcoming, Parliament can reject the proposal outright, so that the Commission can decide whether to drop the matter altogether or revise its ideas.

In this respect, if in no other, the European Parliament can be said to have the last word and the Maastricht Treaty of 1991 increased its powers in another respect when it made its approval necessary before a new President of the Commission could be appointed. In 1994, when John Major blocked the appointment of Jean-Luc Dehaene, this almost caused a crisis when the alternative candidate, Jacques Santer, was approved only by 260 votes to 218. In other respects, however, the Maastricht Treaty made few additions to the powers of the European Parliament. When it added the two new 'pillars' of foreign and security policy and justice and home affairs to the single pillar of social and economic affairs on which the former EEC had been based, no attempt was made to give the European Parliament any real degree of control in these areas. While it has the right to discuss proposals brought forward in both these new areas, it has neither the right to amend them nor to impose a veto.

Until 1979, the European Parliament was made up of members who had already been elected to serve in the parliament of their own country, and who sat on a part-time basis. Since 1979, its 626 full-time members have been directly elected, and sit for a period of five years, coinciding with the period of office of the European Commission. Since German unification in October 1990, Germany has ninety-nine members instead of its original eighty-seven. France would have preferred the number of German members not to have increased, and agreed not to resist the proposal only on condition that the European Parliament continued to meet in Strasbourg.

France has eighty-seven members, as do Italy and the United Kingdom. Spain has sixty-four, the Netherlands thirty-one, Belgium, Greece and Portugal each have twenty-five, Sweden twenty-two, Austria twenty-one, Denmark and Finland sixteen each, Ireland fifteen and Luxembourg six. Except for the United Kingdom, which sticks to the traditional first past the post system, elections to the European Parliament in the other fourteen states are on a proportional representation system.

Currently, the largest group is the Party of European Socialists, with 198 members out of the total membership of 567, followed by the European People's Party, which includes the British Conservative Party, the Ulster Unionists and the French Union pour Démocratie Française, with 157 members, next the European Liberal Democratic and Reformist Group, with fifty-two members, then the Confederal Group of the European United Left with thirty-one members, and the Green Left, with twenty-six members, and various other smaller parties.

Impressive though the variety of these groupings is – there are, in all, ten multinational parties, grouped by political affiliation and not by national origin – the fact that the present European Union has a total electorate of over 250 million people means that members of the European Parliament are elected from constituencies in which there are almost half a million potential electors. Glenys Kinnock, for example, who was elected as an MEP in 1993, represents the constituency of South Wales East, which has an electorate of 454,704. The average size of a British parliamentary constituency is 75,000.

CONTROLS, CHECKS AND BALANCES

The Court of Justice of the European Communities

One of the main functions of the Court of Justice of the European Communities, established by the Treaty of Rome in 1958, is that of deciding whether or not the various treaties have been correctly interpreted. In 1967, the executives of the ECSC of 1951, of the European Community of 1958 and of Euratom were made common to all three Communities, and the Court given jurisdiction over them all.

Just as judgments of the Supreme Court in the United States take precedence on constitutional matters over those of the courts in the individual States, so the decisions of the Court of Justice of the European Communities are directly binding on member states. Its role in this respect is especially important when it is called upon to give judgment in cases where there is a need to establish a precedent in the interpretation of Community law, and thus to apply what Klaus-Dieter Borchart calls the teleological technique: interpreting what the legislators who passed the original law intended it to mean.[7]

It is in this context that the Court of Justice of the European Union is regarded with particular hostility by the Eurosceptics who see British membership of the European Union as an albatross hanging round the neck of a state which is perfectly well able to ensure the rule of law by itself, and without the help of foreigners who, in any case, all owe the original concept to the example of the English-speaking peoples. These Eurosceptics argue that the 'teleological technique' is nothing but the long-standing ability of British courts to establish case law by interpreting Acts of Parliament writ large, and cannot see the need for the existence of a legal body to offer additional rights to British subjects whose freedoms are already fully guaranteed under Common Law anyway.

A possible answer to this criticism is to point out that establishment of the principle of the free movement of workers, discussed in more detail in Chapter 3, was fully achieved only by a series of decisions whereby the Court of Justice of the European Communities required the nation states to recognise that a number of their customs and practices were in fact discriminatory in the effect they had on citizens of other member states. All member states of the European Union have had cases go against them in the European Court, and all have at some time or other had occasion to feel particular annoyance at the fact that where there is a conflict, European law takes precedence over national law.

The Court of Justice of the European Communities, or European Court of Justice, sits in Luxembourg. It is not the same as the European Court of Human Rights, which sits in Strasbourg, and was established in 1950 as a result of the signature of the European Convention of Human Rights. This Court is linked to the Council of Europe, see p. 109, and its task is to protect citizens against all aspects of the misuse of state power. Like the European Court of Justice, the European Court of Human Rights is frequently criticised in the British press. In both cases, however, the British government was a willing signatory to their authority, in the case of the European Court of Justice by the signing of the Treaty of Rome in 1972 and subsequent treaties, and by the signature in 1950 of the European Convention on Human Rights in the case of the European Court of Human Rights.

The rules which originate in the Commission, are approved by the Council of Ministers and the European Parliament, and are subject to interpretation by the European Court, fall into the following categories

* **Regulations**, which are directly applicable in all member countries.
* **Directives**, which bind member states to implement legislation and take other appropriate measures to ensure that the objectives defined in the Directive are achieved.
* **Decisions**, which bind those to whom they are addressed,whether member states, commercial undertakings or individuals.
* **Recommendations and opinions**, which have no binding force, but which show which way the wind is blowing in Brussels, Strasbourg and Luxembourg.

The Court of Justice is the only body entitled to interpret the treaties on which the European Union is founded, as well as the legislation brought forward from the Commission and approved by the Council of Ministers and the European Parliament. It sits in Luxembourg. Cases can be brought to it by the Council, the Commission, or by any other Union body; or by firms, individuals and member states of the Union. Its decisions are binding on all member states, and the Maastricht Treaty of 1991 gave it the additional power to impose fines on member states as well as on firms and individuals. In 1994, one group of firms was fined 248 million ECUs (European Currency Units, roughly £300 million) for infringing articles 85 and 86 on free and fair competition.

The court has fifteen judges, appointed for a renewable six-year term by agreement among all fifteen member states. Once in office, they cannot be dismissed, any more than can the eight Advocates-General. Such a person is, as Michael Swann puts it in *The Economics of the Common Market* (1990), 'a stranger to English legal procedure',[8] but is well-known to most continental systems. Their functions are similar to those of the *amicus curiae*, or friend to the Court, in that they explain to the judges what they believe to be in the best interests of the Union. The judges are not required to follow their advice, but quite frequently do so. The Court can also be asked to deliver what is known in French as 'un jugement préjudiciel', an expression normally rendered by the term Preliminary Hearing. This says what the law would probably be if a certain set of circumstances were to arise and certain actions were to be performed, something which cannot happen in the English Common Law system, which does not take hypothetical cases into account.

In chapter 7 of his book *The European Union: Creating the Single Market* Lord Cockfield argues that the European Community, as it was when he was one of the United Kingdom's two Commissioners between 1984 and 1989

> is an essentially French creation: its philosophical foundation is French; and to this day the working language of the Community is French. It is not surprising therefore that its institutional framework should reflect French political philosophy and particularly Montesquieu's Theory of the Separation of Powers.

In this reading, Lord Cockfield continues

> the Commission is the executive arm of the Community, the parliament and the Council of Ministers share the legislative function; and the Court of Justice in Luxembourg is the judiciary.[9]

This is an instructive way of replying to the objection that the Union is essentially undemocratic because it does not follow the Westminster system whereby the government can be overthrown by a vote in the House of Commons. The machinery whereby the government in France and the United States of America is responsible to the elected legislative assembly may well differ from the conventions prevailing in the United Kingdom. The principle nevertheless remains the same, and in both countries there is a balance of power on the Montesquieu model, with an executive kept rigidly separate from the legislature, and both the executive and the legislative branches of government subjected to the control of an independent judiciary.

The concept of the rule of law is also an integral part of the democratic tradition, and a central feature distinguishing what is called the open society from its totalitarian rivals and enemies. In Hitler's Germany, as in the former Soviet Union and in present-day states such as Iran, Iraq or the People's Republic of China the idea of an ordinary person, or even a privately or publicly owned organisation, making an effective appeal to the law for protection against the misuse of its powers by the state is inconceivable. In the European Union, every person and every organisation, including the European Commission itself, is liable to have its actions called into question by an appeal to the European Court. Chapter 3 gives a number of examples of how this works in practice.

From a cultural as well as from a legal point of view, the establishment of a rule of law applicable throughout the Union is an important part of the European cultural and political legacy. It was in the Roman Republic that the idea of a law which everyone, not only private citizens but also the state itself, was in duty bound to obey, first made its appearance. It is a fundamental principle of the rule of law that there should be a body which finally decides what the law is, and it is hard to see how the European Union could work if there were no authority to take a decision when there is a conflict between the legal systems of two or more member states.

The Court of First Instance

The main function of this Court is to hear cases brought by the European Commission under articles 85 and 86 setting out the rules governing free and fair competition and the need to avoid both the establishment of monopolies and the possible distortion of the rules by the actions of individual member states. An appeal can be made to the Court itself against a judgment made by the Court of First Instance, but only on a point of law. As in the case of decisions made by the Supreme Court of the United States of America, to which the Court of Justice of the European Union is sometimes compared, there is no appeal against a ruling made by the Court itself. The only solution is to try to change the law of the Union, and see that this is applied in future cases.

The European Court of Auditors

This body was established in 1977 on the model of the French *Cour des Comptes*. Like the *Cour des Comptes*, its responsibility is to see that the taxpayer's money is spent in the way intended by the bodies approving the budget. It has access to all the accounts involving expenditure approved under the Union budget, and can make spot checks at any time. As in the case of the *Cour des Comptes*, the Court of Auditors publishes an annual report listing its findings and making recommendations. This report is taken into account by the European Parliament when considering whether to give the Commission formal discharge of responsibility in its management of the Union's budget.

However, whereas the *Cour des Comptes* has the right to require an official found guilty of maladministration to repay any sums of money for which they have legal responsibility, the powers of the European Court of Auditors are more restricted. All it can do is state that a fault has been committed. It has not yet required the other right which members of the *Cour des Comptes* are happy to exercise, that of pointing out how much more cheaply a particular operation would have been carried out if they had been responsible for it.

SUPPLEMENTS, ADVICE AND NUMBERS

The European Council

A possible indication that the Commission and the Council of Ministers do not offer an entirely adequate framework for solving the problems of the European Community, and still need to be supplemented by other arrangements now that it has become the European Union, can be found in the institution known as the European Council. This brings together the heads of government of the member states, and first met in Paris in February 1961. In December 1974, Valéry Giscard d'Estaing, then in his second year as President of the Fifth French Republic, proposed that the arrangement should be institutionalised and meetings have since been held on a regular basis three times a year. Other meetings are held if a particularly serious issue has to be considered. This happened in April 1990, at the time of the first discussions on German reunification, and again in October of the same year to consider the situation after Saddam Hussein's invasion of Kuwait.[10]

The other problems dealt with, however, have been internal to the Community or Union. They include the decision to create the European Monetary System (EMS) in 1978, the final settlement of the problem of the British contribution in 1984, and the agreement of the Maastricht Treaty in December 1991, and the need to continue holding them suggests that the Gaullist idea of 'l'Europe des Patries' is proving remarkably long lived. Such meetings, it has also been suggested, would not be necessary if the Commission and Council of Ministers were doing their job properly. The Ministers are all members of democratically elected governments, and therefore have the delegated power to vote in a way consistent with the views of the government they represent. Indeed, British Foreign Secretaries are required on their return to Westminster to give an account to their colleagues of the way they have voted, and it is hard to see in what way Prime Ministers can be any more representative than Foreign Secretaries of what the government thinks and of the policies they think they can persuade the House of Commons to support.

The Economic and Social Committee and the Committee of the Regions; the European Investment Bank and the European Monetary Institute

The Economic and Social Committee meets in Brussels and has 222 members. These represent various interest groups such as farmers, small- and medium-sized businesses, consumer groups, family associations and ecological movements, and the committee has to be consulted by the

Commission, the Council and the Parliament before decisions are taken in the areas with which it is most concerned. It does not, however, have the right formally to oppose or to propose legislation, any more than does the Committee of the Regions, another consultative body which meets in Brussels.

The Committee of the Regions has 220 members, of whom half are from large regions and half from smaller local authorities. It was established under the Maastricht Treaty of 1991 in order to enable more consultation to take place on the effect of European Union legislation on the various regions of the fifteen member countries, as distinct from its effect on the states themselves. It is particularly concerned with questions such as education and training, social policy, cultural and regional policy and policies affecting cross border links. It does not, however, have an independent budget. The European Regional Development Fund, which absorbs some 30 per cent of the Union's budget, is administered by the Commission.

The European Investment Bank was set up in Luxembourg in 1958 in order to finance capital projects aimed at producing a more balanced economic development within what was then the European Community. It has an annual budget of some 20,000 million ECUs (some £26,000 million), a sum which leads the European brochure *The Institutions of the European Community* to describe it as 'the largest financial institution in the world'. It has an AAA rating (the highest one possible), and lends money for projects in countries outside the Union as well as within the Union itself.

The European Monetary Institute was established by the Maastricht Treaty in order to supervise the preparation for the proposed introduction of the European Single Currency on 1 January 1999. Its headquarters are in Frankfurt, and its governing body brings together the governors of the fifteen central banks of the states in the European Union. Its council meets on a monthly basis in order to assess how preparations are proceeding for the introduction of the European Single Currency.

Numbers

The pamphlet, *Serving the European Union. A Citizen's Guide to the Institutions of the European Union*, published in Luxembourg in 1996 by the Office for Official Publications of the European Communities, begins with the remark that the eight institutions which it describes employ only 24,500 people, less than half the number administering the city of Stockholm.

The fact that 15,000 of these are employed by the Commission is a reminder of how important this body is. Similarly, the fact that 3,000 of these employees are translators and interpreters reflects the problems inseparable from an organisation which now has eleven official languages (Danish, Dutch, English, Finnish, French, German, Italian, Greek, Portuguese, Spanish and Swedish). The other 8,000 employees, of whom, again, about one-fifth are translators or interpreters, are shared between the Council of Ministers, the Court of Justice, the European Parliament, the European Investment Bank, the Economic and Social Committee, the Court of Auditors, the Committee of the Regions, the European Monetary Institute and the European Drugs Agency.

When compared to the 116,139 civil servants employed in 1996 by the Ministry of Defence in Great Britain, the 63,960 members of staff of the Inland Revenue or the 89,960 staff running the Department of Social Security,[11] 24,500 seems at first sight a relatively modest figure for an organisation which plays an important role in the lives of some 370 million people. It would nevertheless be misleading to see this figure of 24,500 as a reliable indication of the amount of administrative work generated by the European Union. A great deal of the legislation approved by the European Union is put into effect by home civil servants working in their own countries.

3 Basic principles

DUTIES, TARIFFS AND TAXES

If the impression given by British newspapers is true, the only reason which the majority of the inhabitants of the United Kingdom see for belonging to the European Union is the negative one of not being faced with the problem of the Common External Tariff when trying to sell their goods on the continent. It is the existence of such a tariff which distinguishes a customs union from a free trade area, and the preference of the British for the latter was made very clear by the attempt in 1960 to establish the European Free Trade Area (EFTA) as a rival and alternative to the European Economic Community (EEC).

In a free trade area, each country abolishes customs duties between itself and its partners, while retaining the right to impose a different rate of duty on goods entering it from elsewhere. In a customs union, which is a higher stage of economic integration than a free trade area, countries do away with customs duties among themselves, and also agree to impose the same rate of duty, known as a Common External Tariff, on all goods entering it from outside, from whatever source. In this respect a customs union represents, as Dennis Swann puts it in *The Economics of the Common Market*, 'a free trade area within a bloc and discrimination against the outside world'.[1]

It is a view which echoes a remark made by Harold Macmillan in 1957 when he justified Great Britain's refusal to join the EEC by describing it as 'a high-tariff group in Europe, inward looking and self-sufficient'.[2] A common market goes further than a customs union, in that the free movement of goods and the maintenance of a Common External Tariff are accompanied by the free movement of workers and capital, and by the freedom to offer services.

For France and Italy, the change in national economic policy involved in the signature of the Treaty of Rome in 1957, and its coming into force on 1 January 1958, represented a more fundamental shift of economic policy than it did for the Benelux countries – Belgium, the Netherlands and Luxembourg – or for West Germany. These states had always favoured a policy of free trade. The two Latin countries, on the other hand, had followed the policy of protecting both their agriculture and their industry behind tariff barriers high enough to bring the price of imported goods to the same level at which home-produced French and Italian products were sold on the home market. If, with the signature of the Treaty of Rome, they still maintained an element of protection against the rest of the world through the Common External Tariff, it was one which ceased to offer them any protection against competition either from each other or from the most dynamic economy of Western Europe, that of West Germany.

In its insistence on removing quotas and customs duties, the Treaty of Rome aimed to establish what are known as the four fundamental freedoms of the European Community. The first of these freedoms, brought about by the taking down of the protective tariffs which had formerly separated the European countries from one another, is the free movement of goods. The second is the free movement of capital, the third the free movement of labour and the fourth the freedom to offer services in all Community countries on the same terms as those applicable to home-based companies. The second of these four freedoms, the free movement of capital, did not increase in so uniform a way as the free movement of goods, and the free movement of labour did not become fully operative until agreement was reached on the mutual recognition of qualifications, and the acceptance on 21 December 1988 of a directive establishing a system of mutual recognition for higher-education diplomas.[3]

In spite of the progress made in abolishing customs duties, which ceased to exist between the six original members of the EEC eighteen months ahead of schedule, on 1 July 1968, it was not until 1 January 1993 that all frontier controls on goods circulating in the European Union finally disappeared. But although technical checks were still being made until that date, goods bought in a shop in a country belonging to what was then known as the European Community have, since 1968, paid no custom duties if they were originally manufactured in a member country. If they have come in from a country outside the Community, they will have paid only the Common External Tariff, an import duty which is the same whatever the country into which the goods were originally imported. With the establishment of the Single Market on 1 January 1993, private individuals may now also buy goods in any European Union country and bring them home without paying any customs duties, provided these goods are for their private use.

Some limitations nevertheless remain, most of them linked to the fact that the member countries of the European Union have retained separate excise duties and continue to impose different rates of VAT, a form of indirect taxation whose basic working can be illustrated in a highly simplified form by the example of a motorist having a repair done to his car. If VAT is levied at 17 per cent, currently the most common rate, then the motorist having a repair costing £100 pays £117. It is assumed – rightly or wrongly, according to the garage – that the repair has added £100 to the value of the car, so that the amount of VAT payable is £17. The same principle is used in calculating the amount of VAT to be levied on manufactured goods and the provision of services, and the system has now almost completely replaced the different forms of indirect taxation which existed before 1958.

An essential element in the fulfilment of the economic and monetary union given as one of the aims of the Maastricht Treaty of 1991 is the creation of a common taxation policy, and the adoption in 1970 by all twelve countries of the EEC of VAT is already an important step in that direction. Administratively, if not politically, it would be quite simple to impose the same rate of tax on all operations throughout the twelve member states, and it is argued by some economists that if the words 'economic and monetary union' given as one of the aims of the Maastricht Treaty mean what they say, a comparable system could and should be extended to direct taxation.

This is nevertheless a highly contentious issue. At the moment, for example, the United Kingdom stands out from its partners by having a zero rate on children's shoes, on foodstuffs and on books and newspapers. There are rational as well as emotional objections to bringing the British into line with the other countries in the European Union, where the VAT rate on such items varies from 5 to 33 per cent, and which would not arise if the proposal were implemented to introduce a uniform VAT rate on motor cars and motor cycles. At the moment, this too varies from one country to another, and anyone buying a car in one country and taking it to be used in another European country has to pay the VAT rate in that state when registering the vehicle for use on the road.

This does not apply to other goods such as washing machines or refrigerators, where anyone living in one of the fifteen states of the European Union can buy them in one state and use them in another, paying only the rate of VAT levied in the country of purchase. Agreement has also been reached for these and many other products as to the technical and safety standards to be observed in the manufacture of such goods. It is the country in which they are made which has to ensure conformity with agreed European norms, and while this has been achieved for radios and electric mixers, it is not expected that uniform standards for cars will be achieved until after 1998.

There are also differences in excise duties, especially between the United Kingdom and France. According to the *European Consumer Guide to the Single Market*, second edition, Office for Official Publications of the

European Communities, 1995, British travellers are advised that the limit is 800 cigarettes, 90 litres of wine, 110 litres of beer and 10 litres of spirit.[4] Such items must have been bought in an ordinary shop or supermarket in one of the member states of the European Union, and not in a duty-free store at a port or airport. They must also be for the personal consumption only of the purchaser, and cannot be sold to a third party. If you have more than the stipulated amount, the customs officer may ask you to explain why, since to have bought such an enormous quantity for your private use might indicate more than a normal capacity for the enjoyment of alcohol. If you can persuade them that 200 bottles of champagne is a reasonable purchase for someone about to celebrate their daughter's wedding or fortieth wedding anniversary, all well and good. If you cannot, you may be suspected of trying to defraud the Excise Commissioners, and be required to pay what you would have paid had you bought the drink in a shop in the United Kingdom, where excise duty is levied in accordance with British law.

There are other limitations. Travellers to Finland or Sweden, including nationals of those countries, are not allowed to take in more than 1 litre of alcohol, 5 litres of wine and 15 litres of beer. Comparable limitations are imposed by Ireland and Denmark, but for each of these countries it is for reasons different from those which might lead a British customs officer to ask questions. Denmark, Finland, Ireland and Sweden are countries which are particularly conscious of the problems created by the excessive consumption of alcohol. Any loss of sovereignty implied by the treaties creating the European Union has not removed the right which member states have under article 36 of the Treaty of Rome to take whatever measures they think fit to protect the health of their citizens.

This right is fully in accordance with the aim of the Single European Act of 1987, which is to complete the process of economic integration by removing the technical barriers which still required goods to be checked at the frontiers between the different states in order to make sure that they conform to certain technical and safety standards. Each member state will, in future, have the responsibility of ensuring that any goods produced on its territory and intended for export satisfy the standards agreed for the whole of the European Union, thus avoiding the need for any further check as they move into another member country.

A crucial step was made in achieving this freedom of circulation by the Cassis de Dijon case of 1979, a dispute which gave rise to a ruling which illustrates the role of the European Court as the body with power to interpret what the Treaty of Rome actually means in disputed cases. The German authorities had objected to the sale of the blackcurrant-based liqueur on the grounds that it did not have the 25 per cent alcohol content required of any liqueur officially designated as such to be legally sold in Germany. The

Court ruled that any product legally manufactured in any one member state could be legally imported into another and sold there under the official name which it has in its home state.

It is easy to see why the free movement of capital took longer to establish than that of the free movement of goods. When the economy of a particular country is weak, because it is importing more goods and services than other countries are prepared to buy from it, the imposition of currency restrictions is one of the ways in which its government can prevent its currency from being sold too widely abroad. It is in this sense that some economists argue that the free movement of capital can be completely achieved only when there is a European Single Currency. This is especially the case when the charges made by banks to convert one national currency into another are normally so high that it is rarely in the interests of a private individual to seek to profit from the lower interest rates in another country by borrowing money there rather than at home, and here again it is argued that a single currency is essential if the free movement of capital is to be meaningful to the ordinary citizen in the European Union.

In 1988, a directive approved by the Council of Ministers established the principle of the free movement of capital, thus putting an end to the situation in many European countries, especially after the war, where both individuals and organisations had to ask permission from their government to take money out of the country, and where countries could take measures to prevent their currency from being freely sold abroad. In the early 1980s, when the policies of the newly elected socialist government led to a fall in the value of the franc as well as to increasing fears for its continued stability, France reintroduced restrictions on the number of francs which its citizens could take abroad with them when they went on holiday. It later sought a derogation from the 1988 directive and did not finally remove all exchange controls until 1991.

After the free movement of goods and the free circulation of capital, comes the free movement of people, especially if they are going to work. All countries, in Europe and elsewhere, have always required anyone going there for anything other than a holiday to acquire special permission if they wish to stay there for a long period, and more especially if they wish to earn money. Even nowadays, some countries outside Europe require anyone visiting them in any capacity whatsoever to obtain a visa – Russia, for example, as well as most of the countries of the Middle East – and every country places strict limits on the right of foreign nationals to come and work there. The Treaty of Rome set out to abolish these restrictions, as far as the citizens of the European Community are concerned, by instituting the free movement of labour. If an Italian wishes to go and work in Germany and can find a German employer ready to employ them, they do not need to acquire a work permit from the German government.

Such a person may, of course, especially if they have gone to work in a country with as well marked a tradition as France of requiring people to be able to prove instantly who they are, be required to obtain a resident's permit to supplement any passport or identity card which they carry from their home country. But unless the country in which the person is going to work can prove that they are a notorious criminal, it cannot refuse them such a document any more than it can refuse an employer the permission to employ any national from another European Community country to whom it wishes to offer work, either on a temporary or on a permanent basis. The principle of the free movement of labour means that a member state of the Community can no more protect its nationals from competition in the labour market against nationals of other Community countries than it can protect its farmers or industrialists against competition from agricultural produce or industrial goods imported from another member state.

All governments have the responsibility of protecting their citizens from possible malpractice by people claiming competence in an area in which they have little or no knowledge. Before anyone can practise as an architect, a doctor, dentist or lawyer, they have to satisfy an official body that they are qualified to do so in their home country. In the past, a foreigner coming into another European country, and wishing to set up as a doctor or lawyer, had to pass the same examinations as a native of that country. Outside the European Community, this is still very often the case and a British doctors going to work in the United States often have to qualify in the state where they wish to practise. In the European Community, matters are made easier by the mutual recognition of qualifications. A Dutch architect or a Spanish pharmacist wishing to go and practise in Italy or Germany, can do so without taking another set of examinations.

Initially, one of the bodies responsible for running matters in the European Community, the Economic and Social Committee (ESC), would look at the subjects which had to be studied, and the examinations that had to be passed. It would then decide, for example, that the examinations enabling someone to become an architect in Italy were basically the same as those not only in Holland, but in all other member states of the Community, and declare that Italian architects could practise anywhere in Europe where they could find work. This was not always an easy process. It took seventeen years to reach the agreement concerning architects and sixteen to arrive at a mutual recognition of qualifications which enabled a pharmacist who qualified in one European Union country to set up in practice in another.[5] Indeed, the complications were such that the practice now in the European Union is to say that someone qualified in one of the fifteen countries is legally entitled to practise in any one of the fourteen others.

The process has indeed been a very gradual one, and it is still the case that fewer Europeans go to work in one another's country than Americans from Illinois go to establish themselves in Texas. There are not many Europeans with a good enough knowledge of the language of another country to go and work in difficult professions such as accountancy or medicine in a country other than their own, and there are also professions which, by tradition if not necessarily by definition, can be exercised in a particular state only by a citizen of that country.

The fifteen member countries of the European Union still have the responsibility of governing and defending themselves, collecting their own taxes and maintaining public order. Since the nineteenth century, civil servants, like policemen or members of the armed forces, have traditionally been nationals of the country in which they work. This has not always been the case, and until the end of the eighteenth century, it was quite common for the kings of France, like certain German princes, to supplement their national armies with mercenaries from abroad. But the idea of national sovereignty, developed in the nineteenth century, has generally come to imply that you have your country run by your own nationals, and in some European countries, this idea has been extended to other professions.

Thus in France, Italy and Spain, as in Portugal and Greece, all teachers at publicly funded educational establishments, at whatever level, are civil servants employed by the state. In the United Kingdom, this has not been the case. Until the establishment of the new Funding Council, teachers in schools or colleges of further education were appointed and paid by the Local Education Authority, and universities have always been independent bodies responsible for recruiting their own staff without any reference to central government. This has contributed to another of the differences separating the United Kingdom from its continental partners, and which has occasionally, created some resentment. For whereas French and German nationals can, if they have the appropriate qualifications, be employed to teach in British schools and universities on exactly the same conditions as their British colleagues, this has not been the case with British teachers going to France, Spain or Italy. Because they are not nationals of these countries, they can obtain exactly the same conditions of service as their French or Italian colleagues only if they become citizens of the country in which they are working and thus qualify themselves to take and pass the examinations open only to those nationals of that country.

This situation is nevertheless changing, and in a way which, like the Cassis de Dijon case, illustrates how the European Court, one of the institutions established by the Treaty of Rome in 1958 and originally known as the Court of Justice of the European Communities, works in practice. As early as 1974, a Dutch lawyer called Reyners wished to establish his right to practise in Belgium. He was fully qualified to do so, in that he had passed all the relevant examinations, but came up against a Belgian rule which restricted the right to practise law in Belgium to Belgian citizens. Dr Reyners appealed against this ruling to the European Court of Justice, which affirmed not only his right to do so but also the general principle that Community law took precedence over national law, especially in the interpretation of the provisions of the Treaty of Rome. By signing the Treaty of Rome in 1958, and accepting the jurisdiction of the European Court, the Belgian government had placed itself in a situation where it had to give way.[6] In 1988, a series of comparable decisions by the European Court extended the right of the nationals of one European country to work anywhere in the Community where they could obtain employment even further by establishing a distinction between civil servants responsible for implementing state policy, or 'protecting the interests of the state', and those concerned with commercial matters or with education.

There is consequently now no requirement that teachers from another member state in the European Community must be citizens of the country in which they take up a permanent teaching appointment. In France, the competitive examinations known as the *Agrégation*, like the slightly less difficult *Certificat d'Aptitude à l'Enseignement Secondaire* (CAPES), were formerly restricted to French nationals. These examinations can now be taken by any citizen from another European Community country whose home qualifications indicate that she or he has already achieved a comparable standard to that of French nationals attempting the examination. If the non-French candidate is then successful, she or he can now be appointed as a teacher in a French school on exactly the same condition as a French citizen.[7]

The fundamental principle of the European Community that Community law takes precedence over national law has thus been extended, at least in theory, from the private to the public sphere, a particularly important event for countries which, like France, have traditionally given both civil servants and the state itself a range of powers and privileges not normally found in English-speaking countries. Where there is a conflict, the national government must give way, and it is cases such as the one affecting the status of school teachers that the limitation on traditional concepts of national sovereignty embodied in the Treaty of Rome is particularly visible, and can be particularly useful to the private citizen. The European Court is there to protect all the citizens of the Community, against their own government if necessary, or against the administrative practices of other countries if the occasion should arise. Had a number of German nationals working as teachers in France and discovering that their conditions of service were less favourable than those of their French colleagues, in that they were not eligible to qualify for permanent appointments on the same basis, not protested about what seemed to them to be a failure to implement the principle of the free movement of workers, it is unlikely that the French educational authorities would have spontaneously changed the rules.

The fourth fundamental liberty which the Treaty of Rome seeks to establish, after the free movement of goods, capital and labour, is that of the free provision of services. Since the services sector is now the biggest employer of labour in the fifteen European Union countries, accounting for over 60 per cent of all jobs, as opposed to 35 per cent in manufacturing, this fourth freedom is in many ways the most important. Only 5.5 per cent of the population is nowadays engaged in agriculture, as against 20 per cent in 1958, and the free provision of services also has important consequences for the consumer. If, for example, a German insurance company is able to offer services on exactly the same conditions in France, Spain or Denmark, as a home-based insurance company and French, Danish or Spanish companies are allowed to do the same in Germany, Great Britain or Greece, then the price of policies tends to come down. German and British insurance companies are, traditionally, more efficient than those in other countries, and one of the presuppositions governing a free market, whether in services or in goods, is that competition will either drive less efficient companies out of a market in which they cannot compete, or will make them bring down their prices to a level where they can.

There is, naturally, nothing new about insurance companies, like banks and stockbrokers, having branches abroad. But in the past, they have been able to establish them only after obtaining permission by negotiations with the host country. Within the European Union this is now an ability which they have of right, though here again problems can arise of a type which parallel those which can still exist even in the United States. Since 1 July 1994, the motorists who takes advantage of the possibility of insuring their car in another European Union country have to pay particular attention to the fact that the degree of coverage may not be exactly the same as the one to which they are accustomed in their own country. They must also take notice of the fact that different European member countries impose a different tax on car insurance. In Denmark, for example, the tax rate is 50 per cent higher than it is in the United Kingdom and in France 33 per cent higher. An insurance company in one European Union country cannot, however, require a motorist to pay a supplement to ensure that third-party cover is valid in all fifteen member states.

Two of the most important articles of the Treaty of Rome are numbers 85 and 86. These specifically forbid any company or group of companies from so monopolising a section of the market that they effectively destroy competition, and the Commission, the most innovative and influential of the institutions established by the Treaty of Rome, has been particularly vigorous in taking companies, organisations and even states considered guilty of unfair competition for judgment by the Court of the Community. In 1989, for example, Brussels airport decided to offer Sabena, the Belgian national airline, a reduction of 18 per cent in airport charges. The privately-owned airline British Midlands protested against the decision, arguing that it gave Sabena an unfair advantage. The Court ruled in favour of British Midlands, and thus against what was in fact a decision made by the Belgian government.

In so doing, it followed a line of argument which was also implemented in 1995, when the Irish Continental shipping company successfully appealed against the attempt by the Chamber of Commerce at Morlaix to restrict the use of the port of Roscoff, in Brittany, to Brittany Ferries.[8] Here again, what was at stake was the right of the consumer to choose the cheapest mode of transport available, and to do so in what the Treaty of Rome calls free and fair competition, a concept more frequently referred to in English as a level playing field. The presupposition is that level playing fields are not only fairer to the companies or organisations competing to offer services. They are also more advantageous to the consumer. Free and fair competition, it is argued, inevitably brings quality up and prices down, and it is even possible that the full implementation of articles 85 and 86, which forbid cartels, monopolies and price fixing arrangements, will finally produce a situation where air travel is as untrammelled by price fixing arrangements within Europe as it is in the United States, thus changing the situation whereby it is, at the moment, often much more expensive to fly from Paris to Rome than from London to New York. By a Council decision of July 1992, an 'open skies' policy for Europe was due to come into force on 1 January 1997, but was postponed until 1 April. The French radio gave the news item full billing in its morning broadcasts, perhaps because all the French airlines went on strike that day. The event was mentioned only very briefly on the BBC, and went without comment in the British press. Although it is too early to tell whether there will be any reduction in fares, the French radio gave prominence to a report that British Airways was cutting costs in order to make itself more competitive. In particular, it was paying its air hostesses and stewards only for the time actually spent in the air, and not for the hours they might have to spend at another airport waiting for their next spell of duty.

If the decision to end the cartel and price fixing which has, up to now, been such a marked feature of the behaviour of European airlines is finally put into practice, it will offer a further illustration of a feature of the

European Union which, at first sight, seems slightly paradoxical. For on the one hand, as was clear from the very moment that the European Coal and Steel Community (ECSC) did not call into question the private ownership of these industries in the countries which had signed the 1951 Treaty of Paris, the European Union to which the ECSC finally gave birth is a thoroughly capitalist organisation. But whereas, in classical Marxist theory, the state performed only a minimal and generally negative role as far as the workers were concerned, being what Lenin called, merely 'the administrative committee for managing the affairs of the bourgeoisie', the supranational authorities established by the Treaty of Rome have come to play a very different role. The Court, Commission and Council of Ministers now constitute an international authority with very far-reaching powers, pursuing what is at times a highly interventionist policy of a type which any organisation seeking to protect the interests of the consumer against those of the manufacturer can only admire.

INTERNATIONAL COMPARISONS AND CONTRASTS

On 19 September 1946, Winston Churchhill gave a speech in Zurich in which he spoke of the need to create what he called 'a kind of United States of Europe'. Even if this ambition is not universally shared, and even if Churchill himself did not see Britain as having more than associate membership of such an organisation, the comparison with the United States of America does offer a useful starting point for defining what the European Union is, and, equally importantly what it is not.

Thus there are, as in the European Union, no customs barriers separating the different states in the United States of America one from another, and no limitations on the right of citizens to travel and work wherever they please. The United States has a single currency, the dollar, whose value is the same in all of the fifty states. If a European Single Currency is introduced, as planned, on 1 January 1999, the parallel between the European Union and this aspect of the United States of America will be even more marked.

The comparison should nevertheless not be taken too far. In the United States, the Federal Reserve Bank decides interest rates for the whole country, and the Federal Government fixes the level of income tax and corporation tax which all citizens and commercial organisations must pay. This is not yet the case in the European Union, though it may happen if and when a European Single Currency is established. Unlike the European Union, the United States has a unified system of government, with the President as Head of State and Commander-in-Chief of the armed forces, a single foreign policy, and a uniform system of Federal laws decided by Congress and interpreted by the Supreme Court.

This is not the case in Europe, and the European Union, like the European Community which preceded it, also lacks many of the other traditional characteristics of the nation state. It has neither an army to defend its citizens against external aggression, nor a police force to protect them from internal disorder. It has not yet developed a common foreign policy, and has, by definition, no common language. There is a European University Institute at Fiesole, near Florence, but this receives only post-graduate students. There are also nine European Schools, one each in Bergen, Culham, Varese, Luxembourg and Karlsruhe and two each in Munich and Brussels which cater for 15,000 of the daughters and sons of employees of the European Union. Programmes with poetic if impenetrable acronyms such as ERASMUS and SOCRATE also enable students from within the European Union to attend courses in other universities, but the wandering scholar has not yet become as frequently a figure as he – and not then she – allegedly was in medieval times.

The European Union does not collect either income tax from individuals or corporate tax from institutions, and has no responsibility for town planning, the upkeep of roads or the security of the coast line. It does, increasingly, try to involve itself in environmental matters, and sets standards for the provision of an adequate water supply. But these services remain the responsibility of national governments, as does also the provision of a health service for its citizens. Although citizens from one European country are entitled to health and other benefits in any one of the other member states, they do so on the same basis as the nationals of that state. British travellers obtaining an E111 before visiting Italy, Belgium or France will be treated in accordance with the health service existing in those countries, not on the same principles which govern the National Health Service. Like education and social security, the provision of a health service remains a national, not a Union responsibility.

The European Union thus does not have a government in the sense that the United States does. All it possesses is a set of institutions. The way these institutions work has been discussed in Chapter 2, and details are given on p. 37 of a possible comparison between the role of the United States Supreme Court and that of the Court of Justice of the European Union. Most of the legal powers which the Union possesses are connected in some way with economics, and its own budget is very small compared to that of even the smallest of the fifteen countries composing it, being not more than 1.5 per cent of their total Gross National Product (GNP). Whereas the United Kingdom spends some £4,500 a year on each of its citizens, the *per capita* expenditure of the European Union on each citizen of the fifteen states composing it is not more than £130.

The comparison with the United States is nevertheless useful on economic as well as political grounds. Economically, it is argued, large markets are more efficient than smaller ones. They have more customers, and can consequently achieve economies of size. The more goods produced by the same process, the cheaper they tend to be. Once the type has been set up, it does not cost much more to run off 20,000 copies of a book than it does to produce 10,000, and the same is true of cars, washing machines, television sets, pocket calculators, types of coal and varieties of steel. Research and development, instead of being repeated and duplicated in several different countries, can be centralised and shared. One of the reasons often given for the prosperity of the United States or of Japan is the size of the domestic market available to producers in these countries. It is this which enables goods to be produced more cheaply for the consumer, partly because of the economies of scale made possible by a large market – 258 million for the United States, 125 million for Japan – partly because the research and development costs are all concentrated in one country.

Thus in the United States, 2.8 per cent of the Gross Domestic Product (GDP) is devoted to research and development, and in Japan 3 per cent. In 1995, in contrast, the total for all fifteen states of the European Union was only 2 per cent. One of the long-term aims of the Single Market, established by the Single European Act of 1986, and which came into being on 1 January 1993, was the creation of a unified economic area able to compete on equal terms with Japan and the United States. The total population of the fifteen states which currently make up the European Union is almost 370 million. This provides the largest group of potential customers in the world and one of the many hopes created by its potentialities is that of raising the amount spent on research and development from its currently rather modest level to a figure higher than that either of the United States or of Japan.

Large markets are also more efficient because goods can circulate without paying customs duties. In the Europe of the 1940s, goods made in one European country could not normally be sold outside that country without being checked by the customs and paying the levy set by each country importing them. One of the first achievements of the six countries signing the Treaty of Rome on 25 March 1957 was to succeed, by 1 July 1968, in removing all customs duties between them. It showed how sensible the decision had been in the early 1950s to begin the creation of a united Europe in a relatively small way. Rather than start in a grand, ambitious manner and try to fuse the economies and political systems of all the different European countries into one single market by one single decision, the statesmen of France and the Federal Republic of Germany began with two industries which were complementary, whose centres of production were geographically close, and which had a similar role to perform in the economy of their respective countries.

It is a result of the process begun by the creation of the ECSC in 1951 that custom posts between the fifteen countries of the European Union (Austria, Belgium, Denmark, Finland, France, Germany, Greece, Ireland, Italy, Luxembourg, the Netherlands, Portugal, Spain, Sweden and the United Kingdom) have been virtually abolished. Goods travel from Ireland to Germany, from Italy to Denmark or from Portugal to Finland, with no more formalities than they do in the United States when they go from Texas to North Dakota, or from California to Massachusetts; that is to say, none at all.

Another similarity with the United States of America lies in the possibility that all forms of passport control on the borders between the fifteen member states of the European Union will eventually disappear. This would also fulfil the dream expressed in 1945 by the Foreign Secretary in Clement Attlee's Labour government, Ernie Bevin, when he said that the aim of his foreign policy was to enable anyone who wanted to do so to go down to Victoria Station, buy a ticket to wherever they wanted, and go there straight away. This is not yet possible in every sense as far as citizens of the European Union are concerned, in that frontier posts are sometimes still there, and travellers can still be stopped and have their documents checked. But the long waits at the frontier posts separating France from Spain or Italy are now a thing of the past. If one does not yet have the same possibility of always driving from Germany into France with the same total freedom of any check being made on one's movements as is enjoyed by the traveller entering California from Oregon, the day does not seem too far off.

It was this total freedom of movement which was one of the ambitions of the agreement signed by France, Germany, Luxembourg and the Netherlands on 25 March 1995 at the small town of Schengen, in Luxembourg. They were joined later in 1995 by Italy, Spain and Portugal, when they also decided to adopt a common policy on the granting of visas to nationals. One obvious disadvantage of this aspect of the Schengen agreement was that it expected all the member states of the European Community to have the same policy towards countries with which each had very different visa and immigration relationships.

What the Schengen agreement originally meant was that any traveller entering Europe from a 'Third Country' such as Australia, Algeria, Brazil, Burma, Canada, Zaire or South Africa, would have to go through the formalities of immigration only once. Once their credentials had been checked at whatever port or airport at which they entered the European

Union, whether it be Hamburg, Paris or Lisbon and they had been admitted into Germany, France or Portugal, there would be no check on whether they then went to Italy, Spain or Greece.

Such travellers would not, unless they obtained special permission, be able to work in one of the countries of the European Union. They would still not be citizens of a member state, and would not therefore be able to benefit from articles 3, 8 and 48 of the Treaty of Rome establishing the principle of the free movement of workers. But their freedom to move around in Europe was intended to parallel the free movement created for agricultural products or industrial goods which had paid the Common External Tariff and were thus circulating freely in the Community. The full implementation of the Schengen agreement would thus have had what many might consider the advantage of making the European Union even more like the United States, where anyone holding a visa to visit can travel freely to any one of the fifty states in the Union without any further checks on their identity to supplement those carried out at the port of entry.

A practical objection to the full implementation of the Schengen agreement nevertheless came from the police forces in the European Union. Frontier posts are very useful in the fight against crime. A number of countries on the continent of Europe have not succeeded in eliminating rabies. Now that the Channel Tunnel has made travel between France and Great Britain so easy, it still seems reasonable to carry out health checks on animals entering the United Kingdom. The Netherlands have a more liberal attitude to drugs than either France or Belgium, a fact which has recently led France to invoke the safeguard clause in the Schengen agreement by maintaining spot checks on all travellers coming into the country, whether citizens of a member state of the European Union or nationals of a 'Third Country', especially if they are coming in from the north and north east. The computer technology enabling information to be sent from one police force to another has not yet reached the stage where information suddenly obtained by the German police can be sent to every port of entry into the European Union fast enough to prevent a suspect individual coming, for example, into Portugal, and thus securing the right theoretically available under the Schengen agreement to travel right up to Finland without any further check on their identity or motives.

However, Denmark and the United Kingdom indicated from the very beginning that they would not implement the Schengen agreement, and thus insisted on their right, as sovereign states, to maintain control of who crossed their borders. Except in war time, citizens of the United Kingdom have never carried identity cards, and even those issued between 1939 and 1945 did not carry the photograph which is an integral part of the identity cards which citizens of France, Spain, Italy or Germany must be able to produce when asked by the police to prove who they are.

This absence of identity cards is partly a result of the suspicion of the power of the state which has been a feature of British life since the seventeenth century, and partly an illustration of the practical advantages of being an island. Since it was easy for the immigration authorities to check on who was going to come into the country, there was much less of a case for giving the police the power to stop people in the street and ask them to prove their identity. Public opinion surveys of attitudes towards the European Union tend to show the British as most sceptical of its advantages, and most suspicious of those aspects of it not directly related to the purely economic advantages which it is said to offer. For the Eurosceptics, the Schengen agreement has two disadvantages: it makes it too easy for people to come into the United Kingdom; and it makes the introduction of what are seen as essentially un-British institutions such as the identity card seem more probable.

NATIONS, ATTITUDES AND RESERVATIONS

The continued and widespread use in Great Britain of the term 'common market' to refer to what since 1 November 1993 has officially been known as the European Union emphasises the tendency on this side of the channel to look solely at the economic advantages or disadvantages of British membership. This attitude is in marked contrast to that of the Spaniards and Portuguese, who see the European Union as a means whereby they can be integrated into Europe, and finally put an end to the old jibe that Africa begins at the Pyrenees. The existence in Spain of a strong regional tradition, exemplified by the strength of the movement for Catalan independence and the vigour of the Catalan language, also means that there is a keen appreciation of the way in which what is called the 'Europe of the Regions' can reduce what has often been seen as the excessive power of the central state.

There is less enthusiasm in Greece, where elements within the Socialist Party have retained something of the same hostility towards what they see as an essentially capitalist Europe, which parallels that of the British Labour Party until the late 1980s. However, the fact that Greece is the poorest of the fifteen current members of the Union creates a lively awareness of the advantages of the regional fund. Memories of how the military government of the colonels made Greece ineligible for membership between the *coup-d'état* of 21 April 1967 and their removal from office on 7 July 1974 provide support for membership of an organisation whose members have to be parliamentary democracies respectful of human rights. This is accompanied by the fear that if Greece were to leave the Union, her place might be taken by Turkey, whom she is most unwilling to see as a member.

There is also, in the attitude of the other members towards Greece, something of the same awareness of a historical debt which helps to explain why there is less hostility than might have been expected towards the United Kingdom. Since it has been not only a reluctant applicant but also a visibly self-interested one, Great Britain has remained what Stephen George's 1990 book calls, *An Awkward Partner*,[9] and seems likely to remain so. However, since it was the behaviour of Great Britain between 1940 and 1945 which alone enabled a democratic Europe to survive, there is a residual sympathy for this country which has still not quite disappeared. Similarly, when Greece became the tenth member of the EEC, in 1981, the event had a symbolic as well as political significance. It was in fifth-century Athens that the traditions of intellectual tolerance, scientific curiosity, philosophical speculation and political democracy, which are the defining characteristics of European civilisation, had first shown themselves.

The reservations felt in Greece and Great Britain have no equivalent in Germany, where European integration has always been seen as a means of rejoining the family of civilised nations which the Third Reich so tragically abandoned between 1933 and 1945. Membership of the European Community has also, for the Germans, always been a way of linking their fortunes with those of Western Europe, and thus of avoiding the temptation to look eastward for allies. It was a tendency that showed itself in the Rapallo pact of April 1922, by which Germany became the first European power to establish commercial and diplomatic relations with the régime established in Russia by the revolution of 1917, before producing more disastrous results when the August 1939 non-aggression pact between the Third Reich and the Soviet Union helped to spark off the second world war. In Italy, European political integration has also been seen as a means of escaping from the period which began in 1922 when it became, under Mussolini, the first country to adopt a fascist dictatorship. An appreciation of the advantages of European membership has also been made more intense by an awareness of the imperfections of political life in Italy itself, as well as by the absence of a strong sense of national identity stemming from the fact that the country did not achieve unification until 1859.

For the French, especially after their withdrawal from Algeria in 1962, the movement towards a more unified Europe has been a means of reasserting their role as a power whose influence transcends their national borders. Indeed, de Gaulle himself is reported as saying in 1962 that Europe was 'the means for France to become again what she has not been since Waterloo: the first in the world',[10] and the attitude which this ambition has inspired has not always made France the most comfortable of partners. The

Fouchet plan of 1962, developed before the period when de Gaulle was to incur considerable unpopularity by his two vetoes on British entry, as well as by the 'empty chair' policy of 1965, sought to replace the unifying role of the Commission by a committee which would sit in Paris and reach agreement by negotiations between national civil servants representing their home state. Not even the advantages which French agriculture has obtained from the Common Agricultural Policy (CAP) have prevented the rise of a Eurosceptic movement, associated as in the United Kingdom with the political right as well as with the extreme left, and which gave rise to the extremely narrow majority by which the referendum of September 1992 ratified the Maastricht Treaty.

The Dutch and the Belgians, together with the inhabitants of Luxembourg, have always seen themselves as being at the forefront of movements towards European integration. In January 1948, they signed a treaty providing for the free movement of goods, services, capital and labour between the three countries, and showed how their identities could be further merged by a name which they gave themselves: the Benelux countries (Belgium, the Netherlands, Luxembourg). Bernard Connolly interprets the attitude of Eire to the European Union in his characteristically uncharitable way when he writes in *The Rotten Heart of Europe* (1995) that

> For Irish politicians, influence over the allocation of money from the Structural Funds meant keeping a grip on the levers of influence, patronage and power in Ireland's parish-pump political world

and describes these politicians as feeling that their careers 'depended on the European pork barrel'.[11] Other observers are readier to understand why a country which has suffered so much at the hands of the English should be so enthusiastic in grasping the opportunity of asserting itself by establishing links with the continent of Europe which are free of any involvement with the political traditions of the Catholic church, and which offers so many opportunities for general economic improvement. What is perhaps even more surprising is that the workings of the CAP have, in the case of Eire, not led to the same kind of rural depopulation to which they have given rise in France, Italy or parts of the United Kingdom. Indeed, by the support which the CAP has provided for the mixture of dairy and cattle farming which characterises Irish agriculture, it has brought new life to many country areas threatened with decline.

The British are not entirely alone as members of the European Union in thinking that their own brand of politics has little to gain from closer association with Europe. Just as the Danes, Swedes and Finns see themselves as belonging to another cultural and linguistic tradition, that of the Scandinavian countries, the British are highly conscious of how their links with the English-speaking world of North America and Australasia make them different from the other countries of Western Europe. The Finns, it is true, have a political motive in belonging to the European Union which is comparable to that of Germany. Both countries have memories of how uncomfortable it was to be close neighbours of the former Soviet Union. But like Great Britain, none of the Scandinavian countries have memories of a home-grown totalitarian or dictatorial movement comparable to the one which triumphed in Germany with Hitler, in Spain with Franco, in Greece with the colonels, in Portugal with Salazar, in Italy with Mussolini, and which was able to establish itself with disquieting ease when the defeat of 1940 led the French to accept the authoritarian and anti-semitic Vichy régime of Marshal Pétain.

4   Contested practices

AGRICULTURE, SURPLUSES AND PROTECTION

The Common Agricultural Policy (CAP) is an aspect of the Community which explains why it should be so frequently referred to as the Common Market. There is a common market in agricultural produce in that fruit, vegetables, meat, milk, butter, cheese, cereals and wine circulate freely from one European country to another without paying customs duties. The French farmer producing peaches or tomatoes cannot, by the imposition of a tariff which makes fruit and vegetables from outside France more expensive than home-grown produce, expect to sell goods more cheaply than a Spaniard or an Italian farmer exporting produce into France. If they wish to compete, they must sell goods of better quality at a lower price, and the CAP has never meant uniform prices for the consumer in all the different member countries. It is the farmers who receive the same guaranteed minimum price, whatever the size of the farm and whatever country they inhabit.

The goods that circulate freely among the fifteen nations of the European Union, so long as certain standards of hygiene and safety are observed, include peaches, pig meat and poultry, as well as calculators, cars and clocks. Agricultural produce from outside the Community, on the other hand, like industrial goods, such as television sets from Japan, cars from the United States or furniture from Sweden, has to pay the Common External Tariff. This tariff is the same whether the goods come in through Amsterdam, London, Naples, or Athens, or whether they come from countries such as Chile or China, Uruguay or Argentina. It varies according to products, not by point of entry or country of origin.

The Common External Tariff creates a sense of political as well as economic identity in that it defines the economic relationship of each member state to the outside world in exactly the same way. In the absence of a common foreign policy, which is still in an embryonic stage, it provides the beginning for a Europe unified in its relation to all the states which the language developed in Brussels defines as 'Third Countries', a category which is simple to define, consisting as it does of all countries which are not members of the European Union.

Tariff barriers have two main functions: they provide income for a state by requiring importers of goods to pay duty on them before selling them on the home market; and they provide protection for domestic products against competition from abroad. None of the fifteen member states of the European Community have ever relied heavily on customs duties for their national income. The main purpose of the Common External Tariff, which must be paid on all goods entering the area covered by the European community is a protective one, and this is especially the case as far as agricultural produce is concerned.

For climatic as well as other reasons, it is still more expensive to grow wheat in Italy or England than it is in Canada or the United States, more expensive to raise sheep in France than in Australia, dearer to make butter in Holland than to import it from New Zealand. The only way in which important sections of European agriculture can be economically viable is consequently by imposing customs duties on products from overseas in order to prevent them from being cheaper, and thus more attractive to the consumer, than food grown within the boundaries of the Community. In order to fulfil the ambition of article 39 of the Treaty of Rome to 'ensure a fair standard of living for the agricultural community', protection is essential.

In Act 2 of *Macbeth*, the porter includes among the inhabitants of Hell 'a farmer who hanged himself on expectation of plenty'. If the weather is too good, an agricultural system efficient enough to grow enough food in a poor year will inevitably produce surpluses. Farmers who cannot then get an economic return on their produce because competition has forced prices down run the risk going bankrupt. The CAP avoids this danger by offering farmers a fixed price for their produce. This stimulates them to grow enough to satisfy demand, while guaranteeing them a specific price, defined in advance, for anything they cannot sell on the open market.

The money to pay the guaranteed price for agricultural produce is naturally lower than the farmer would normally hope to get on the open market, generally known as the target price, and does not offer spectacular profits. Indeed, as was underlined by the demonstrations by French farmers in the autumn of 1991, it can be so low as to reduce cattle farmers to virtual penury. If the disaster of a hot summer follows an exceptionally dry winter and spring, such farmers have to spend so much money buying fodder for their cattle that they make no profit at all. The guaranteed price nevertheless saves European farmers from the modern equivalent of having to 'hang himself on the expectation of plenty': selling their products at so low a price that they have to borrow even more money from the bank.

The money to make up the difference between a low market price and the higher guaranteed price is provided by the European Agricultural Guidance and Guarantee Fund (EAGGF), sometimes still known by the French acronym, FEOGA, (Fonds Européen d'Orientation et de Garantie Agricoles). The EAGGF, or FEOGA, receives this money from the contributions which the fifteen member states pay to the Union out of the income which they receive from the taxes levied on the goods imported or consumed by their citizens, and from the import duties paid on agricultural produce and industrial goods entering any of the member states from 'Third Countries'.

The CAP has been criticised on four main grounds. First of all, it is accused of guaranteeing farmers too high a price for their produce, and thus creating inordinately large surpluses and costing the tax-payers in the Community a great deal of money. Second, since the more a farmer has to sell, either at the target or at the guaranteed price, the greater the profit, it has favoured the large producer rather than the small one. Third, the CAP is said to have turned the European Community into a rich man's club. The poorer countries of the developing world find the European market closed against them, since their lower production costs, which would normally have allowed them to sell at a competitive price in Europe, are not reflected in the higher price at which the Common External Tariff compels them to try to sell their products within Europe. Fourth, by offering export subsidies to European farmers who wish to sell their produce abroad, the CAP enables European farmers to sell their goods at the lower, world price outside the Community. This leads, in the view of the critics of the CAP, to a policy of dumping, or selling produce at below cost price, which again works against the interests of the developing world.

Moreover, as the Americans argue, the CAP policy distorts world trade by preventing genuinely free competition. Farmers everywhere, they maintain, suffer from the unfair advantage which the Europeans have given themselves. Not only has the CAP given European farmers a captive home market in which they have no incentive to compete with more efficient farmers from abroad, and are thus not encouraged to reduce their costs and the price of food to the consumer. This policy has also, in the view of its critics, created an excessively powerful trading bloc which tries to fix prices for the whole world. By preventing the food that can be produced more cheaply outside Europe from entering the protected zone, it also keeps food prices in the Community artificially and unnecessarily high. Even after the reforms of the mid-1980s, it was calculated by the French economic historian J-M. Jeanneney that the Community price for wheat was 53 per cent above the average world price, for butter 175 per cent and for sugar 200 per cent.[1]

In reply, the supporters of the CAP point out that the surpluses, never more than 5 per cent of the total production, are much better than the shortages still characterising the agricultural system of Russia and Eastern Europe, and which were a defining feature of the planned economy developed in the Soviet Union after 1917 and imposed on its satellites after 1945. Supporters of the CAP also remind their critics that the Union does, through the Lomé Convention, signed in 1975 when it was still the European Economic Community (EEC) with over 70 countries from Africa, the Caribbean and the Pacific, offer developing countries an entry into the European market for most of their agricultural products. These supporters point out that the Community buys three times as much agricultural produce from the United States and from developing countries than it sells to them, and that American farmers receive comparable subsidies from the United States government to enable them to sell their produce abroad.

Supporters of the CAP also find themselves attacked from within the Union itself, in that the policy which they are defending is criticised by farmers and fishermen for providing inadequate protection against competition against imports from 'Third Countries'. French farmers block the roads and destroy agricultural produce in transit on the grounds that the authorities responsible for the imposition of the Common External Tariff have not done their job properly. French farmers also complain that this tariff is much too low, and are especially sceptical of the lamb imported into France from the United Kingdom, arguing that it really comes from New Zealand, and therefore ought not to be there at all. At the same time, the British press is particularly critical of the Common Fisheries Policy, which it sees as having been unnecessarily tacked on to the CAP, and presents it to its readers as a characteristic example of the basic mistake which the British government made in the first place when it signed the Treaty of Rome and accepted the jurisdiction of the Court of Justice of the European Communities.

Thus one of the measures agreed in the 1983 reform of the CAP involved a number of limitations of the principle of equal access of all Community states to European waters. This went some way to satisfying British objections by re-affirming the principle that each member state had the right to a 12-mile exclusion zone around its coasts, which was reserved for nationally-owned vessels or traditional users. However, the principal competitors of the British fishing fleet, the Spaniards, then began to get round this by registering their vessels in British ports, and an attempt was made to prevent them from doing this by the 1988 UK Merchant Shipping Act. This placed restrictions on the number of foreign vessels which could register in British ports, but proved vulnerable to an appeal made in 1991 by the Spanish fishermen to the Court of Justice of the European Communities on the principle of non-discrimination on the grounds of nationality set out in article 7 of the Treaty of Rome.

The appeal, under what is known as the Factortame case, was successful, and the British government had to give up this attempt to protect the interests of its fishermen against what they saw as unfair competition. The owners of the Spanish boats which were impounded before the European Court gave its judgment in the Factortame case are now appealing against the loss of earnings which they suffered by not being allowed to use their boats, and the case has been referred by the European Court to the High Court in London. If the Spanish fishermen are successful, the British government will be liable to pay out a sum which varies, according to the newspaper one read, from £40 million to £80 million and even, according to *The Daily Mail* of 11 September 1996, either £80 million on page 8 or £150 million on page 15. In the end it was fixed at £30 million.

Supporters of the European Union point out in reply that the rules of the Common Fisheries Policy apply to everyone, and that French and Spanish fishermen make exactly the same objections to its operations as do the British. They also draw attention to a parallel between what they see as an excessively nationalistic approach to the problems of the Common Fisheries Policy and the circumstances which give rise to racial attitudes in individual nations. Such attitudes, they maintain, recur most frequently in shortage areas such as jobs and housing. If, they also contend, the seas around the coasts of Europe – and, indeed, the seas everywhere in the world – were not suffering from centuries of over-fishing, the problem would not arise. In their view, disputes over fishing rights are not the creation of the Common Fisheries Policy. They go back to the 1960s and the 'cod wars' which took place between Great Britain and Iceland, and which were the product of the unilateral creation by the Icelandic government of a 200-mile zone around its coasts which excluded British fishermen from the grounds which they had fished traditionally.

In February 1997, two British-based publications gave opposing views of the fishing dispute which provide a microcosm of the debate about the United Kingdom's membership of the European Union. *News*, the paper put out at his own expense by Sir James Goldsmith's Referendum Party and sent free to every household in Great Britain, contained an article by Christopher Booker under the title 'This Secret Deal Betrayed British Fishermen'. This argued that when, in 1970, Sir Edward Heath was preparing for the negotiations which led to Britain's entry into the European Community in January 1973, he fell into a trap designed by its six original members. Realising that fishing rights would, within a few years, be extended to 200 miles around all coastal waters, they 'cobbled together' a regulation giving every member state a right of 'equal access' to everyone else's fishing waters. This meant, as Christopher Booker put it, that 'British waters containing four-fifths of the fish became a "common European resource"', and the 'first part of the trap was sprung'.

This was followed, in 1983 according to Christopher Booker, by the establishment of the Common Fisheries Policy which Great Britain was required, as a member, to accept. This, Christopher Booker argues, gave Great Britain 37 per cent of the 80 per cent of the fish which she 'really owned', and the situation was made worse in 1986 by the arrival of Spain, 'the cuckoo in the nest', with her 'vast fishing fleet and a reckless contempt for conservation rules'. Since the rules of the EEC gave Spain equal access to community waters, more and more Spanish boats were allowed, as Christopher Booker to put it, 'register under the British flag to grab a share of our quotas'.

It is slightly surprising that Christopher Booker should not have supported his argument by using one of the points made by Richard Barry in his article 'Hopping Mad' in the February 1997 issue of the monthly magazine *Prospect*. For what Richard Barry reports is that when, in 1970, the EEC established the Common Fisheries Policy, each state was given a quota based on the catch which it had declared during the previous year. However, when the quotas were subsequently allocated for the period 1973–1978, after Britain's entry, the British fishing industry was honest in declaring how many fish had been caught, while the other states followed their normal practice of declaring catches that were 'grossly inflated', a fact which explains the figures of 80 and 37 per cent quoted by Christopher Booker.

However, Richard Barry points out in his *Prospect* article, there are in fact only 140 quota-hopping vessels fishing from British ports out of a total of 2,900 boats of over 10 metres in length, and the regulations do not apply to boats smaller than this. Of this, 140, some two-thirds are Spanish, the others being mainly Dutch and French and Richard Barry makes two other points to support his general argument that although quota hopping is a serious local issue it is

> not important enough to jeopardise the vital principle of equal access for our business through the EU, or to put the nation at yet more humiliation at the hands of the other 14.[2]

His first point is that the principle of equal access to Union waters cuts both ways, and that Shell's subsidiary in Spain has successfully found and extracted oil near Valencia for many years. His second point is that the majority of boats not originally based in Cornwall, one of the areas said to be worst affected, and which are claimed to be driving Cornish fishermen out of business, are not from Spain but from big fishing companies in Scotland.

Like other Eurosceptics such as Bernard Connolly in *The Rotten Heart of Europe*, Christopher Booker writes in an emotive style which does not always make his arguments more convincing. Again like Bernard Connolly, he imputes bad faith, dishonesty and incompetence to those who hold the opposite view. The banner headline to the first edition of *News* read

THEY LIED THROUGH THEIR TEETH

while in *The Rotten Heart of Europe*, Bernard Connolly describes Jean-Claude Trichet's *Dix Ans de Désinflation Compétitive* (1992) as

a compound of crass errors in elementary economic reasoning, flagrant contradictions, cant and misrepresentations of other economies.[3]

Criticisms of British membership of the European Union, and especially the participation of the United Kingdom in the CAP, are frequently accompanied by the argument that while the British authorities are zealous in their enforcement of European regulations and directives, their European equivalents are not. The argument that we play the game, even against our own interests, whereas foreigners cheat is a difficult one either to prove or refute, as is also the accusation that the CAP gives rise to an extraordinary amount of fraud. This may well be true, but at least it can be pointed out that the European Community, as it then was, tried to remedy this situation as long ago as 1977 by the establishment of the Court of Auditors. It is its annual report which provides much of the information on which the allegations of waste and fraud in the CAP are based.

Another defence of the CAP is the somewhat paradoxical one of saying that it is not really very important, since the price support for agricultural products which it provides absorbs only 0.5 per cent of the Gross National Product (GNP) of the European Union as a whole. It is true that this represents a larger share of the total Union budget than all the other Union activities put together: 51 per cent, as against 32 per cent for regional and social aid, 6 per cent for aid to the developing world, 5 per cent on administration, 3.5 per cent on research and development and 2.5 per cent on industry and education.[4] The European Union has also agreed, from 1995 onwards, that it will reduce its financial support for agriculture by 20 per cent over a period of five years. This is in keeping with its long-term hope of making European agriculture as independent of subsidies as any other activity in the Union such as the manufacture of motor cars, clothes, furniture or washing machines.

The social and ecological cost of trying to make agriculture totally self-sufficient is considerable. It has led to the situation in which farming has become industrialised, especially in the Netherlands and parts of East Anglia, while other areas of Europe, especially parts of Wales and central and south west France, have suffered severe depopulation. This is nevertheless not a problem for which the CAP can be held to be solely responsible. Already, in 1760, Oliver Goldsmith was issuing his lament on the decline of the traditional English countryside and writing, in *Sweet Auburn*,

Ill fares the land to hastening ills a prey,
Where wealth accumulates and men decay;
Princes and lords may flourish, or may fade;
A breath can make them as a breath has made;
But a bold peasantry, its country's pride,
When once destroyed, can never be supplied.

A flight from the countryside seems to be an inevitable consequence of industrialisation wherever it occurs, just as a desire to escape from what Marx called 'the idiocy of rural life' remains a permanent desire of young people born into what they regard as the narrow environment of a small village. It would naturally be possible, by a general change of policy, to slow down the drift from the land. The tax-payer's money could be used to support small farms, and to subsidise more amenities in the countryside. But this would require the tax-payer's agreement, which might not be forthcoming.

The CAP causes more disagreement with the United States than any other aspect of European Union policy, with its defenders pointing out that the United States itself spends large sums of money buying up surplus meat and butter produced in America, and keeping it in expensively refrigerated conditions. Although this disagreement is unlikely to end quickly, there have been improvements. Since 1973, when it took part in the Tokyo round of negotiations under what was then the General Agreement on Tariffs and Trade, one of the roles of the European Commission has been to represent the interests of all member countries in international commercial negotiations. The final result of the 1990 Uruguay round of talks on possible reductions of tariff barriers and export subsidies was an agreement whereby the European Union reduced its customs duties from 6.8 to 4.1, and the United States brought its down from 6.6 to 3.4 per cent. Since the average level of customs duties throughout the world in 1947 was around 40 per cent, this was a considerable achievement.

It is unlikely, given the immense productivity of scientifically organised farming in the advanced industrial world, and the difficulty of planning for such a vast industry, that the problem of surpluses will ever disappear. But in this respect, as its supporters insist, the only real defect of the CAP is to have been too successful. In 1958, people still remembered a time when the

Dutch, at the end of the second world war, had suffered from a famine so severe that they ate the bark off the trees. One motive inspiring the CAP – to enable Europe to feed itself – was in this respect so obviously important that it scarcely deserved mentioning. As in the political aim of the Treaty of Paris of 1951 establishing the European Coal and Steel Community (ECSC), the avoidance of war between France and Germany, the initial aim has been so successfully achieved that most observers have forgotten that a problem ever existed.

One of the main reasons why the United Kingdom did not join the European Community in 1958 was the traditional British preference for a cheap food policy, and it is still the British who most frequently voice the criticism that the CAP makes food too expensive. In the middle of the nineteenth century, the British began to feed their rapidly increasing population mainly with food imported from abroad, especially from Australia, Canada, New Zealand, the West Indies and the United States, paying for it by exporting the industrial goods in which the United Kingdom then led the world.

This food was much cheaper than most of the produce which could be grown at home, but there was no protective tariff. The cheap food imported from abroad would have driven all but the very largest British farmers out of business had it not been for the system of deficiency payments. This involved the use of the money which the government obtained from the whole of the tax-paying population in order to provide farmers with an income which supplemented the otherwise inadequate payment which they received from the sale of their crops.

The system kept British agriculture sufficiently alive for it to be able to expand as rapidly during the 1939–1945 war, as it had between 1914 and 1918, and thus help feed a population threatened with starvation by the German submarines. Its supporters also defended it on the grounds of social justice, arguing that a high price food policy, such as the one established by the CAP, is harder on the poor than on the rich. A person earning £25,000 and paying £1 for a loaf of bread has much more money left after this essential purchase than one earning only £10,000 and paying the same price.

It is indeed much fairer to the poor to use a proportion of the taxes paid by the rich in order to subsidise the farmer to grow cheap food, since it is the poor who will derive most benefit from such a policy. The farmers, it is true, lose the satisfaction of earning their living by selling what they grow. In the demonstrations regularly organised by French farmers, one of the most frequent complaints is that the guaranteed price which they are receiving for their products is so low that it requires them, once their bills have been paid, to live on direct personal hand-outs from the state, and that this is not a humiliation which they are prepared to accept.

The matter nevertheless looks very different from the point of view of the British consumer, who regrets the disappearance of the cheap food policy, and there is another aspect to the argument about food prices which anticipates some of the reasons behind the British refusal, in 1991, to accept the Social Chapter of the Maastricht Treaty. A country which succeeded in maintaining a cheap food policy while its competitors were having to buy food at a much higher price is benefiting from a form of wages subsidy which might well, other things being equal, enable it to produce industrial goods at a much lower cost, and thus to lay itself open to the charge of practising unfair competition.

Having failed, in the negotiations leading to its entry in 1973, to maintain the subsidy to wages involved in the low price of the food imported from the Commonwealth and from the United States, the British government is also seen by its partners and rivals as providing a different way of keeping wages low by refusing to implement the Social Chapter. Together with the other social benefits accompanying it, this aspect of the Maastricht Treaty was said in an article in *The Daily Telegraph* of 3 September 1996 to add £44 to every £100 of the cost of labour in Italy and £32 in Germany, while the cost of providing less generous benefits enables employers in the United Kingdom to keep this addition to their wages bill down to £18.

LEGISLATION, AID AND THE FREE MARKET

On 15 October 1988, Mrs Thatcher told the Conservative Party Conference at Brighton that

> we have not worked all these years to free Britain from the paralysis of socialism only to see it creep through the back door of central control and bureaucracy in Brussels [5]

and her speech inspired the formation of the Bruges Group of academics, politicians and journalists hostile to what they saw as the threat to Great Britain's national independence in the provisions of the Maastricht Treaty of December 1991.

One member of this group, Martin Holmes, went so far as to write in *The Times Literary Supplement* for 24 May 1996 that 'the Europe of Maastricht is just as doomed as the Europe of Napoleon and Hitler'. For xenophobic Englishmen with long historical memories, his remark recalls Bonaparte's attempt between November 1806 and his defeat in 1814 to ruin the commercial power of Great Britain by the Continental System. This sought to exclude all British goods from the markets of continental Europe, and one of the great fears of Eurosceptics who would like to leave the European

Union but do not dare to suggest it openly is that a similar barrier may be erected in the future.

Martin Holmes's remark was nevertheless as tactless as Nicholas Ridley's 1993 description in *The Spectator* of the European Union as 'a German racket for taking over Europe', and he made what was perhaps the more effective point when he commented that the United Kingdom had, since 1986, accumulated a deficit of £105 billion with the countries making up the European Union, as opposed to a trade surplus of £13 billion with the rest of the world.

In her speech to the Conservative Party Conference, however, Mrs Thatcher was also thinking of the large number of regulations approved by the authorities in Brussels and imposed on the member states. There are indeed an increasing number of these, and the passion for legislating which is said to have always characterised the European Community sometimes makes it look rather silly. One particular legend is that Directive 7–241 on the harmonisation of chocolate recipes will require British manufacturers of chocolate to call their product vegolate on the grounds that it does not contain enough cocoa fat. Another is that animal welfare regulations will require shellfish in transit to be watered every eight hours, another that the design of the British double-decker bus will have to be altered by the provision of a second staircase. Another, especially popular in Denmark, that all ships, of whatever size, are to carry 200 condoms, together with an accusation formulated in Finland that the European Commission wishes to harmonise the temperature of water in private as well as in public swimming pools.[6]

There was even, on 20 August 1996, a report in *The Daily Telegraph* to the effect that Rolls Royce cars would no longer be able to have their characteristic grid on the front of the bonnet. Statistics collected by the European Commission suggested that some 700 lives could be saved a year if vehicles had rounded rather than square edges. However, a spokesman for the company gave the reassurance that 'we always comply with legislation', and did not anticipate any problems in complying with the proposed Transport Directive for Pedestrian Friendly Car Fronts. The most visible way in which the European Union plays a part in the economic process is by introducing legislation aimed at protecting the consumer, laying down standards for safety in areas as different from one another as children's toys, cosmetics, medicines, contracts, the labelling of goods and hygiene standards in the serving of food.

However, few of the interventions which Brussels carries out aim to bring about a planned economy on socialist lines. Indeed, its actions often have the effect of reducing the power of the nation states belonging to the Union to play a decisive role in the running of their own economy. In June 1993, for example, the European Commission was successful in requiring a number of major state-owned undertakings, including the French car maker Renault and British Aerospace to pay back the financial aid which they had received from the French and British governments.[7] This was in keeping with the basic idea inspiring articles 85 and 86 of the Treaty of Rome, which is that companies manufacturing goods which are in competition with similar goods produced elsewhere in the Community all do so on equal terms, with no state being allowed to give one of its industries an advantage over a competitor in another state either by direct subsidies or by the provision of special tax arrangements.

In socialist economic theory, it was axiomatic that the state should have control over what Harold Wilson once called 'the commanding heights of the economy'. This would enable it not only to give help to industries which it felt were particularly important to the general economic well-being of the nation, but also to direct investment in a way which it felt was appropriate. This might well involve, as was illustrated by the action of the French socialist government in 1981 in taking thirty-nine major banks and other credit institutions into public ownership, thus ensuring that investment policy came under the direct control of the state, and it would be hard to imagine a socialist government accepting the modern tendency to give independence to a state central bank.

The European Union, in contrast, like the EEC which preceded it, is based much more on the idea that the most efficient economic system is one where market forces operate in free and open competition, with the role of the state being limited to ensuring that the rules of the game are equally observed by all parties. The state may, it is true, give help to regions which are geographically or structurally disadvantaged. This is nevertheless not the same as offering subsidies to individual companies, or taking them over in order to finance them with the taxpayer's money. It is also difficult to see evidence for creeping socialism in the fact that most of the interventions of the European Union seek to protect the legitimate interests of workers and consumers. If the arrangements for bringing in a European Single Currency go ahead as planned on 1 January 1999, there will be another similarity with the world's leading capitalist power, the United States of America, in the role given to the Independent European Central Bank. Just as the Chairman of the Federal Reserve Bank in the United States is not obliged to do what the President tells him, so the European Single Currency will be run by a committee of twelve bankers who will be equally able, if they think fit, to act in a way of which their national governments do not necessarily approve. If this is what is meant by allowing socialism to 'creep in again by the back door', then the European Union again seems to have a funny way of doing it.

The aim of the Social Chapter is to offer rights and advantages to all workers such as freedom of movement, equal treatment for men and women, increased opportunities for vocational training, improved working conditions and better health protection in the workplace, the right of association and collective bargaining, the rights of the elderly and the disabled, increased consultation of workers and better protection for children and adolescents. It might, in this respect, be seen as interventionist, in that it presupposes that conditions of employment should take account of other factors apart from market forces. But it does not impose a minimum wage, which is a feature of national economic policy in countries such as France and Germany. It leaves the nation states free to decide on the best way of ensuring that workers as well as share-holders benefit from the increased prosperity which the single market, operating in other ways on strictly capitalist lines, is said to bring with it.[8]

After the CAP, which continues to absorb almost half of the money spent by the Union itself, as distinct from the sums spent by the individual member states, it is the Committee of the Regions which receives the second largest share of the budget, some 31.5 per cent. This budget itself remains relatively modest. It is not more than 0.03 per cent of the total Gross Domestic Product (GDP) of all fifteen member states, and in this respect the European Union is scarcely a financial leviathan. But it is a frequent experience, as one drives round countries such as Ireland or Greece, or visits the less well-developed parts of France, Italy or Great Britain, to notice how many projects are being funded by the European Regional Development Fund.

The EEC also sought to establish a common policy on transport, energy and foreign policy as well as on agriculture, and these still form part of the long-term plans of the European Union. In the United Kingdom, it is the tachometer, the instrument which registers the distance and time a lorry has been driven, which is an aspect of the Common Transport Policy that has attracted most public attention, as has also the imposition of a uniform axle weight for goods vehicles which is mostly higher than the one normally thought advisable by British drivers. But road policy differs considerably from one country to another, with access to motorways in the United Kingdom and the autobahns in Germany being free, France and Italy requiring motorists to pay a toll to use the auto-route and autostrada, and subsidies for the state-owned railways in France being much higher than for train operators in Great Britain.

CONTRIBUTIONS, ARGUMENTS AND REFERENDA

The economic arguments in favour of Britain's membership have always been finely balanced. In 1971, when the question of Britain's application for membership of the Community was being debated in the British press, *The Times* published two letters, side by side, each signed by the same number of equally eminent economists. One letter said that it would be in Great Britain's best interests from an economic point of view to join the Community, the other said it would not.

A rising tide, it is argued, raises all boats, and it is possible that the improvements which have gone on in the European as well as in the British economy since the end of the second world war might have taken place anyway. The two essential steps in post-war recovery were the Marshall Aid Programme of 1947 and the decision of the United States to pursue a programme of intensive rearmament. The former ensured that Western Europe would benefit from the wealth of North America, while the second provided exactly the right boost to ensure that the economy of the United States did not relapse into the depression of the 1930s. The Cold War ensured that France and Germany would forget their differences anyway in the face of what seemed, at the time, so terrifying an enemy. The general reduction in tariffs which has occurred over the last thirty years might well owe a good deal to the example of the EEC. It could nevertheless have happened anyway, with the same beneficial impact on the world economy.

The heretical notion that the improvements attributed to the 1951 Treaty of Paris and to the 1957 Treaty of Rome would have taken place even if the EEC had never existed is not widespread. What has been more frequently suggested is that the habit of international co-operation in financial matters is now so well-established that it does not need to be supported by the elaborate administrative framework of the European Union. British Eurosceptics who voice this suggestion also contend that the financial cost of belonging to the European Union is too high, and maintain that membership of a European Single Currency will increase it still further.

This is particularly the case, they argue, because of a basic difference between the way in which money has been put by for pensions in Great Britain and in the other fourteen member states. Whereas British employees have tended to belong to a company pension scheme, and have therefore put by collectively some £600 billion, nothing comparable has happened in the Continent. There, it is the state alone which has tended to collect money to pay retirement pensions, and has done so on a grossly inadequate basis. The result of this is a deficit of £26,000 for each insured person, compared to little over £1,000 in the United Kingdom. Since one of the essential features of the single currency is the requirement that countries taking part in it pool their currency reserves, and thus harmonise their indebtedness, they maintain that each man, woman and child in the United Kingdom will, if we participate in the single currency, have to pay £20,000 to support the pension schemes currently in operation elsewhere in Europe.

These figures are taken from Sir James Goldsmith's *News*, and should perhaps be treated with caution. There has nevertheless been a forerunner to this quarrel about pensions in the form of the dispute which came to a head in the early 1980s about the contribution which the United Kingdom was required to make to the central budget of what was then the EEC. The British argument, put forward with some vigour by Mrs Thatcher, who was Prime Minister at the time, was that Great Britain made a disproportionately high contribution to the budget of the Community, especially if the rate of such contributions were to be seen as reflecting the country's GDP.

She maintained, in other words, that because Great Britain had become a poorer country than France or West Germany, she should pay a lower contribution. This contribution was, however, like that of the other member states, calculated in a way which made Mrs Thatcher's arguments vulnerable to a certain amount of criticism. For each country's contribution is calculated in the same way: as a percentage of the Value Added Tax (VAT) collected within the country, together with a proportion of the agricultural levies and duties on industrial goods received for goods entering a member state from a 'Third Country' and thus paying the Common External Tariff. Other member states argued that there was a simple reason why the British contribution was so large: the United Kingdom continued to import a higher proportion of its food from 'Third Countries' such as Australia, Canada and New Zealand, and was thus out of step with the general policy of Community preference. If, it was suggested, the United Kingdom were to observe the principle of Community preference, and took more apples and wheat from France, and more butter, bacon and cheese from Holland, the problem would not arise. Mrs Thatcher did not agree, and it is a measure of the residual popularity which Great Britain still enjoys in Europe that she was finally successful in getting what she wanted.

The solution updated an arrangement whereby Great Britain was to receive a regular rebate on her VAT contributions which would compensate for the high level of agricultural levies which she paid, the sum involved being some 1.35 billion ECUs (European Currency Units), or roughly £1 billion at the then rate of exchange. It was an honourable compromise, though one which underlined the advantages which Europe as a whole has derived from the fact that the Germany which signed the Treaty of Rome in 1958 did so from a position of moral inferiority explicable by the fact that only thirteen years had gone by since the collapse of the Third Reich. In 1993, her net contribution to the European budget was £9,210 million, compared to Great Britain's £2,433 million and France's £794 million.[9]

It was in a way appropriate that it should have been François Mitterrand who did most to bring about the solution to the problem of Britain's contribution. In 1995, Robert Gibson translated his own expression of 'la mésentente cordiale' by the phrase which forms the first part of his study *The Best of Enemies. Anglo-French Relations since the Norman Conquest.* Like the term 'la mésentente cordiale', the phrase 'the best of enemies' underlines the extent to which the rivalry and hostility between France and England stem from the fact that we are in many ways so remarkably similar. Neither of us particularly likes the idea of a Europe in which the nation state will lose more and more of its power to a series of international institutions. De Gaulle's behaviour between 1958 and 1969 made it clear how well-founded the rumour was that France had accepted majority voting when the EEC came into being in 1958 only because she was temporarily too weak to resist it, and fully intended to replace it by 'l'Europe des Patries' as soon as possible. Great Britain has always held a similar view, and if neither country has been successful, it has not been for want of trying.

Suspicion of the European Community has indeed been a cross-party phenomenon in the United Kingdom, with only the most obviously virtuous party, the Liberal Democrats, being wholly in favour. The Wilson government which took over when Edward Heath lost the General Election of 1974 was much less enthusiastic than Mr Heath had been about membership of the Community. It insisted on renegotiating the terms of British membership and on 5 June 1975 held a referendum to ask the British people if they really wanted to stay in the Common Market. Although 67 per cent of those who voted said yes, only 36 per cent of the electorate bothered to turn out, and the majority might have been smaller if the increase in the cost of food which was one of the results of the CAP had not been overlaid by the very high rate of general inflation, which reached 25 per cent in 1977.

It was not in fact until the late 1980s that the British Labour Party began to be enthusiastic in its support for the European Union. The election of Michael Foot to the leadership of the Labour Party in 1980 marked a general move to the left, and in 1982 a commitment to withdraw from the European Community became official party policy. Together with withdrawal from the North Atlantic Treaty Organisation (NATO) and unilateral nuclear disarmament, this was one of the policies under which the Labour Party fought and lost the General Election of 1983, and in the General Election of 1987, the attitude of the party to what was still called the European Community was decidedly ambiguous.

In the 1989 elections to the European Parliament the Labour Party fully endorsed British membership, and differentiated itself from the Conservative Party by calling for a full implementation of the Social Chapter. This may have helped the Labour Party to win more seats than the Conservatives in the European election of 1989, and thus to give the grouping of socialist parties an overall majority in the European Parliament. Neil Kinnock's present position as one of the United Kingdom's two

European Commissioners, with particular responsibility for Transport Policy, nevertheless, represents a considerable change in personal attitude of a man who had been a Labour MP for Bedwelty since 1970, a member of the National Executive since 1979, and Leader of the Party from 1983 to 1992. It also reflects a change in general policy which has produced the surprising effect of making the Labour Party of Tony Blair appear to be more obviously in favour of the European Union than the Conservative Party of John Major.

The break-up of the Soviet empire in the early 1990s, after the opening of the Berlin Wall on 9 November 1989, has meant that a number of other states which consider themselves to be culturally and historically part of Europe have been allowed to apply for membership of the European Union and to sign transitional agreements with it. These include Poland, Hungary, the Czech Republic and the Slovak Republic, as well as Romania, Bulgaria, Estonia and Latvia. If the success of a club is measured by the number of people wishing to join, the European Union is the political success story of all time. There is nevertheless a case for saying that there are some problems, especially the proposal to create a single currency, which it needs to solve before accepting any further members, and it is the nature of these problems which forms the subject matter of the fifth and final chapter.

5 Currencies and power

THE DOLLAR, TAXES AND THE SNAKE

The Treaty of Rome contained no reference to economic and monetary union and did not mention the introduction of a single currency. These are aims which were developed and adopted later, and the meeting of the European Council of Ministers at Maastricht in December 1991 set out a timetable whereby the currency now known as the Euro would be established not later than 1 January 1999. A monetary union exists, obviously, in the United States of America, where the dollar has the same face value in Maine, Michigan and Missouri, and where nothing prevents a businessperson in New York from investing his or her money in New Mexico or New Orleans. If the piecemeal approach to European integration adopted from 1951 onwards by the six founder states of the European Community succeeds in creating a singe currency, this will offer another similarity with the United States.

Since the implementation of the Single European Act in 1987, there have been no restrictions on the free movement of money among the fifteen member states. Belgians can buy Greek drachmas, Irishmen Dutch guilders, Frenchmen pesetas or Englishmen Deutschmarks, without even telling their government what they are doing, let alone having to ask permission from a central bank. They naturally incur bank charges, just as travellers still do when they move from one country to another in the European Union, and a British journalist anxious to illustrate the possible advantages of a single currency once set out from London with £1,000, changed it into an equivalent sum in each of the fifteen member states, and came back with only £330 in his wallet, without having actually bought anything to use, eat, drink or wear, or paid anyone to do anything for him except change his money. The arguments for and against a single currency are nevertheless more finely balanced than this example suggests, and Bernard Connolly, attributing the anecdote to Leon Brittan, currently one of the United

Kingdom's two Commissioners in Brussels and to Roy Jenkins, President of the European Commission between 1977 and 1981, makes the pertinent comment that it was a rather unusual thing to have done.[1]

Supporters impatient at the delay in introducing a single currency can draw comfort from the fact that it was not until 1913 that the US Congress established a proper Federal Reserve System to stabilise and guarantee the value of the dozen or so types of dollar in circulation. Supporters of a single currency might also like to draw attention to the view that the economic development of the United States was considerably hampered in the nineteenth century by the absence of a genuinely common currency.[2]

The first attempt to create greater monetary stability in Europe took place in 1972, when France and the Federal Republic of Germany proposed the creation of what rapidly became known as the 'snake in the tunnel'. This was an image which expressed the way that all the currencies of the Community would vary together in their relationship with the dollar, rather as a snake might go up and down beneath the ground as it moved along inside a tunnel. Each currency varied in its relationship to the others, but never went outside the skin of snake as the group of currencies went up and down.

The decision to try to prevent the currencies of the European Economic Community (EEC) from varying too much with respect to one another, and to try to stabilise their relationship with the dollar, was taken in response to two events which occurred outside Europe. The first of these was the announcement by President Nixon, on 10 August 1971, that the United States would no longer guarantee the exchange value of the dollar as the world's major reserve currency. The second was the decision of the Organisation of Petrol Exporting Countries (OPEC), in October 1973, to quadruple the price of oil. The rise in the price of oil heightened the inflationary pressures and monetary uncertainty already produced by what had in fact been a devaluation of the dollar, and made the attempt to create a zone of monetary stability in Europe an even more obviously useful measure.

President Nixon's decision had been brought about by the refusal of the United States of America to finance the war in Vietnam by increasing taxes, and to do it by printing money instead. The oil increase was part of an Arab attempt to blackmail the United States and Western Europe into ending the support for Israel so that the Egyptians and Syrians could fulfil what was then their stated aim of destroying the State of Israel. If the attempt to stabilise the currencies within the EEC was part of an attempt to create a kind of 'fortress Europe', it was one which did not seem unjustified at the time. Some of the reservations expressed about the decision taken at the Maastricht conference to introduce a European Single Currency on

1 January 1991 stem, in contrast, from the feeling that there is no correspondingly immediate need to make such a radical change.

In 1972, the limits within which the countries taking part in the snake were to allow their currencies to vary were relatively narrow. A currency wishing to stay within the snake was not allowed to vary by more than 2.5 per cent above or below a central line. This remained the basic idea in 1978, when it was again France and the Federal Republic of Germany which took the initiative in proposing the creation of the European Monetary System, the EMS. The British refused to take part when this system was established in March 1979, and thus to link the value of the pound with that of the other currencies of the European Community.

A country belonging to this system undertook not to allow its currency to rise or fall in value by more than a certain percentage in relation to a central pivot. The value of this central pivot could vary in relation to other currencies such as the yen, the American or Australian dollar or the Swiss franc. If the Deutschmark was in demand, the central pivot – the European Currency Unit (ECU) – went up more than if the drachma or the Irish punt did; but these currencies had to follow the upward movement of the Deutschmark. The influence which a currency had was known as its weighting, which depended in turn upon the Gross National Product (GNP) of the country issuing it. The GNP of France is higher than that of Portugal, and so the French franc had a higher weighting than the Portuguese escudo, and played a proportionately higher role in determining the value of the ECU in relation to other world currencies. Since the Gross Domestic Product (GDP) of the Federal Republic of Germany was higher than that of any other individual country in the EEC, the Deutschmark played a larger role than any other currency in determining the international value of the ECU.

The system underwent a fundamental change in the summer of 1993, and the fact that currencies were then allowed to vary by ± 15 per cent in their relationship to the central pivot, and still remain officially part of what is also known as the European Exchange Rate Mechanism (ERM), is an indication that the system is not working quite as was intended. Before then, a country which was a member of the ERM and found that its currency was falling more than by a certain percentage in relation to the ECU (± 2.5 per cent if it was the narrow band, consisting of Germany and the Benelux countries, ± 5 per cent if it was in the broader band, as France was), it was obliged to stop this happening. One way for a country to protect its currency has always been for the central bank to create a demand for this currency by buying it itself, using the other currencies which it has in its reserves in order to do so.

Alternatively, or in addition, the government may increase interest rates so that foreigners will wish to buy the currency in question because they will get a higher rate of return on their holdings. Or again, a government may accompany this increase of the rate at which individuals or organisations may borrow money by reducing public expenditure in the hope of bringing down the rate of inflation and thus making its currency more stable, and therefore more attractive to investors. In theory, other Community countries belonging to the ERM could also be expected to show support by buying the currency in question. However, if its currency was becoming too valuable, a country was expected either to sell it, or to take other measures such as an expensive programme of public works which would bring its value down to within the agreed band.

The system allowed a certain flexibility, in that a country could request a re-evaluation of its currency if it found the going difficult. Thus in 1981, a socialist government came to power in France with a programme of economic reforms which involved a considerable increase in government expenditure. There was nothing in the rules of the European Community to prevent France from moving away from the more orthodox economic policies which had tended to be adopted during the first twenty-three years in the life of the Fifth Republic, and in that respect France's membership of the European Community had in no way diminished its right to order its own economic affairs as it wished. But its action in shortening the official working week to thirty-nine hours, increasing the minimum wage, improving social security benefits, and creating more jobs in the civil service led to a considerable rise in the purchasing power of the average French citizen.

This produced an increased demand for consumer products which French industry could not supply, but which foreign countries, both within the EEC and in the outside world, were only too delighted to satisfy. This, inevitably, led to a weakness of the franc, which illustrated the law of supply and demand by falling in value in relationship to the other currencies which its citizens needed to buy, albeit indirectly, in order to purchase the German cars and Japanese television sets which they had suddenly found themselves able to afford.

The decline in the value of the franc led the French government, in October 1981, June 1982 and again March 1983, to ask for what was in fact a devaluation of its currency. Details of these events are given in the Chronology, from which it is seen that the devaluation of the franc was accompanied by an official increase within the ERM of the value of the Deutschmark and the guilder, currencies whose increasing attractiveness were reflections of the success of the German and Dutch economies.

The existence of the ERM, and France's continued membership of it in spite of her economic difficulties, nevertheless made this devaluation very different from previous ones, and especially the one decided on 10 August 1969, when France suddenly devalued the franc by 6.6 per cent. It is true that everyone knew how much the French economy had been weakened by the Grenelle agreements negotiated on 27 May 1968 by Georges Pompidou and which increased the purchasing power of the average worker by some 10 per cent. This increase had been made in order to dissuade the trade unions from supporting the student rebels who were seeking to overthrow de Gaulle's government, but also had the inevitable consequence of an upsurge in the demand for imported goods.

Although this provided a foretaste of what was to happen when the election of François Mitterrand in 1981 had given the French socialists the opportunity to put their economic theories into practice, the way in which the devaluation was announced was quite different. In the days of fixed exchange rates, when the value of a currency remained constant and did not move up and down within a system, it was important for a government not to tell anybody what it was going to do. If it did, then other countries would immediately start to buy or sell the currency, thus removing any competitive advantage obtained by a surprise devaluation.

It was often possible to see this devaluation coming, as when Harold Wilson devalued the pound in September 1967 from $2.80 to $2.40, promising that its value would remain the same in people's pockets and blaming its fall on the international currency speculators whom he dubbed the Gnomes of Zurich. But it too, like the French devaluation of 1969, was a unilateral decision, taken without consultation with other countries, and intended to take everyone completely by surprise. When, in contrast, the franc was devalued in October 1981, June 1982 and March 1983, it was after prior consultation between France and those of her partners who were in the ERM, and by agreement among them.

INFLATION, UNEMPLOYMENT AND THE ERM

The impossibility of knowing what other countries were going to do was an additional factor in creating an uncertainty about exchange rates which the existence of fixed parities had been supposed to avoid. When the ERM was introduced, the changes were quite accurately referred to as readjustments. They took place as a result of a general agreement which meant that any change in the value of an individual currency within the ERM did not wholly destroy the long-term confidence in the ability of the system to produce greater stability in exchange rates.

One of the advantages of this stability is that businesspeople can decide to expand by building new factories, knowing that if they order material from another European country, it is not suddenly going to cost 13 per cent more in their own currency than expected. Monetary stability also tends to bring inflation rates down to the level of the European Community country with the strongest economy, and it was partly for this reason that the British government decided, in November 1990, to go back on its ten-year-old refusal to link the value of the pound to that of the other currencies in the ERM.

In so doing, the British accepted, albeit only temporarily, the same limitations on their national sovereignty under which the Belgians, Danes, Germans, French, Italians and Irish had lived since 1979, the Greeks since 1981 and the Spaniards and Portuguese since 1986. The severe punishment imposed on forgers, even at a time when the resale value of the gold or silver which made up the actual physical coin was as great as that of its face value, expressed the monarch's displeasure at having the royal monopoly infringed. Only the monarch had the right to issue coin of the realm.

In the twentieth century, the ability to control the money supply – the modern equivalent of the coin of the realm – is one of the most important ways in which a government can influence the behaviour of the national economy. If it raises the bank rate, it makes it more expensive for firms and private individuals to borrow money. This discourages consumers from buying goods on credit, and businesses from raising loans to install new machinery. What the French call 'le privilège régalien de battre monnaie', and which modern economists describe as the ability to control the money supply, is seen in the modern world as one of the most important attributes of national sovereignty.

The refusal of the British government, until November 1990, to enter the ERM was in this respect a sign of its attachment to the Gaullist idea of 'l'Europe des Patries' as opposed to the Federal Europe now accepted as a legitimate aim by a number of other Community countries. It was a political gesture, expressing an attitude which went right back to the United Kingdom's initial refusal to involve itself with the European Coal and Steel Community (ECSC) in 1951, and the decision to leave the ERM on 'Black Wednesday', 17 September 1992, is sometimes presented in comparable terms. The British government, it is argued, has regained the ability to order the economic affairs of the country in the way it chooses, and in keeping with the needs of the British economy. It does not have to adjust the value of its currency to keep in line with a general policy whose results do not particularly matter to the United Kingdom.

Economists favourably inclined to the idea of economic and monetary union tend to see the embarrassing emergence of the pound from the ERM on 17 September 1992 more as a result of a wrong decision as to the rate at which sterling entered the system than as a pointer to the faults of the system itself. They suggest that it was unrealistic to have gone in at 2.93 Deutschmark to the pound, at a time when the United Kingdom inflation rate was running at over 7 per cent while the average for the Community as a whole was 5.5 per cent. Exchange rates, they argue, should not be used as a means of controlling inflation, which was one of the reasons used to justify the entry of the United Kingdom into the ERM in November 1990. They should be seen as a reflection of the general strength of the economy. A country where inflation is running at a higher rate than that of its neighbours, and whose economic performance is generally weaker, cannot hope to keep its currency at the same level as its more efficient rivals. Such a country's currency is bound to decline, for the simple reason that people will sell it, knowing that in a year's time it will be worth correspondingly less than a currency which is not losing its value at a comparable rate through inflation.[3]

Had the United Kingdom gone in at 2.40 Deutschmark to the pound, it is argued, it might have managed to stay the course, especially if the general political situation in Europe had been more stable. But as had happened in the early 1970s, the economic problems of the United Kingdom were compounded by a number of events which took place elsewhere. Although these events had nothing to do with the British economy, their deleterious effects became increasingly unavoidable because of Great Britain's membership of the Community, and more especially of the ERM.

The first and most important of these events was German reunification. The fall of the Berlin Wall on 9 November 1989 led to this reunification taking place with remarkable speed, so that on 3 October 1990, Germany became one country again for the first time since 1945. But this reunification meant that the German Federal Republic, whose dynamic economy had been a major factor in creating the prosperity of the EEC, was increasingly preoccupied in trying to bring the economy of the former East Germany up to the level of the West. Because of the runaway inflation of the 1920s, which in 1923 had seen the value of the Deutschmark fall to one million millionth of its 1913 value, the Germans had retained a vivid awareness of the danger of allowing the money supply to get out of control. After all, it was the inflation of the 1920s, as much as anything else, which had created the circumstances which enabled Hitler to come to power. The West German government did not therefore wish to bring the standard of living of the 13 million inhabitants of the former German Democratic Republic up to that of their fellow citizens in the West simply by pumping more money into the system. They consequently kept interest rates relatively high, thus making the Deutschmark even more attractive to overseas investors than it already was, and thus greatly strengthening it in its relationship to the pound.

There was also, in 1992, the political uncertainty associated with the ratification of the Maastricht Treaty. The Danish 'No' in the referendum of 2 June 1992, by the narrow majority of 50.7 to 49.3 per cent, set off a wave of currency speculation in which, as the author of 'The Official View of the Bank of Spain' puts it in Paul Templeton's 1993 collection *The European*

Currency Crisis, 'almost all ERM currencies depreciated against the Deutschmark'. Spain was obliged to devalue the peseta by 5 per cent on 16 September 1992 and later by 8 per cent on 13 May 1993, before becoming one of the countries whose currency was to move into the ± 15 per cent band on 2 August 1993.[4] On 18 May 1993, the Danes held a second referendum in which they said 'Yes' by a majority of 58 per cent, prompting the comment by Eurosceptics that the European Union had limited faith in democratic procedures which did not produce the result it wanted. If you did not give the right answer the first time, they said, this merely exposed you to the risk of being asked the same question again until you said 'Yes'.

By the time the results of the first Danish referendum were known, however, the damage had been done, and the general uncertainty about the political future of what could officially become the European Union only when the Maastricht Treaty was ratified, was compounded in the summer and autumn of 1992 by the uncertainy about the result of the French referendum on Maastricht due to be held on 20 September. The difficulty which the pollsters had had in predicting the result became fully explicable when the 'Yes' vote was finally only 51 per cent of those voting, another indication that the 'ever closer union' defined in 1958 in the official Preamble to the Treaty of Rome was more difficult to achieve than the other moves towards a unified Europe which had followed one another with such apparent inevitability since 1951.

British Eurosceptics add to their general reservations about Maastricht the view that it was a mistake for the United Kingdom to have joined the ERM in the first place, and contrast the improvement of the British economy since September 1992 with the problems still persisting in the economies of those countries in continental Europe which have remained within the system. Unemployment in the United Kingdom they point out, has fallen to 7.6 per cent, in contrast to the situation in France, where in early 1997 it was more than 10 per cent, and in Italy, where it went up to 12.2 per cent. Even in what has always been thought of as the power house of Europe, unemployment in Germany reached 4.5 million in March 1997, the highest total since the 1920s.

Explanations for the high rate of German unemployment vary according to the views of the commentator as to whether or not it is a good idea to try to introduce a single currency on 1 January 1999. Commentators favourable to such a currency stress the difficulty which Germany is still having in bringing the economy of the former East Germany up to the level of the more prosperous West. Once the problems associated with German re-unification have been solved, they argue, it will be a relatively easy matter to introduce the single currency in the form envisaged.

Those who are opposed to the Maastricht criteria for the introduction of a single currency point out in contrast how dangerous it has proved to impose such a series of straitjackets on an economy which was already moving into recession because of the high interest rates judged necessary to avoid the inflationary effects of reunification. The attempt to satisfy these criteria, they maintain, will continue to make it impossible for a long time yet for Germany to solve the economic problems of reunification.

Although scepticism about the proposed introduction of a single currency is probably more widespread in the United Kingdom than anywhere else in Europe except perhaps Denmark, there is no particularly intense enthusiasm for it among ordinary people in either France or Germany. In France, the high level of unemployment is seen as a consequence of the government's refusal to stimulate the economy by abandoning the policy of *le franc fort*, and there is quite widespread reluctance in Germany to run the risk of replacing the traditionally strong Deutschmark by what may well turn out to be a weaker currency. Since the 1950s, the great advantage for the average German of having a strong Deutschmark is that it makes holidays elsewhere in Europe, and indeed in the rest of the world, remarkably cheap. This is not an advantage which many voters are anxious to surrender.

It is nevertheless only in the United Kingdom that there is so much outspoken hostility to a single currency. This is supported by the fact that its opponents tend to speak of 12 September 1992 not as Black Wednesday but as White or even Golden Wednesday. Exports increased, thanks to the competitive advantage obtained by a weaker pound, and the economy grew faster than that of any of its three major continental competitors, France, Germany and Italy. The supporters of the discipline imposed by the ERM said that this was all a flash in the pan, and maintained that there would be tears before bedtime as the inflationary effects of devaluation caught up with the United Kingdom as they invariably had in the past. In reply, the Eurosceptics point to the generally poor record which economists have had in predicting what is going to happen, and maintain that the improvement in the British economy since 1992 is living proof of the advantages to be derived from a country's freedom to manage its own affairs without interference from abroad or the need to take the interests of other countries into account.

SCHUMAN, THUCYDIDES AND MR MICAWBER

At first sight, the problems encountered by the ERM in 1992 and 1993 do not provide a favourable background for the proposed introduction of the European Single Currency, scheduled for 1 January 1999. The history of European unification since 1951 nevertheless offers a number of examples of quite surprising recoveries after major setbacks, as when France's rejection of the European Defence Community in 1954 offered a challenge taken up by the creation of the EEC three years later, or the effects of the oil crisis of the 1970s were overcome to the point where more and more countries wanted to join the Community.

There is also some encouragement to be drawn from past precedents in the fact that the clause in the Maastricht Treaty of December 1992 giving the date for the introduction of a common currency on 1 January 1999 sets a number of clearly defined conditions for a country wishing to take part. The Treaty of Rome itself had some very precise objectives, with a carefully planned timetable, and experience does seem to show that progress towards European unification is best achieved by the setting of precise and definable targets rather than by the statement of general principles. This was certainly the way Robert Schuman saw matters when he said on 9 May 1950, when presenting the idea of the ECSC to the press, that

> L'Europe ne se fera pas d'un coup, ni dans une construction d'ensemble; elle se fera par des réalisations concrètes créant d'abord une solidarité de fait [We shall not make Europe by one single stroke, or by building it in one piece; We shall create it by a series of practical achievements, by actions which create the actual experience of sharing].

The method which he and Konrad Adenauer adopted in 1950 has certainly worked better than the more grandiose projects entertained by thinkers in the 1920s and 1930s such as Salvador de Madariaga, José Ortega y Gasset or Richard Codenhove-Kalergi and politicians like Aristide Briand.[5]

Eurosceptics, however, tend to think in different, less charitable terms. For them, the practical, step by step approach which also formed part of Jean Monnet's approach to European unification is uncomfortably similar to the salami tactics whereby Mr Krushchev, during the Berlin crises of 1959 and 1961, tried to whittle down the rights of the Western allies to keep their troops in West Berlin. First of all, he tried to insist that their aircraft did not fly above 10,000 feet in the air corridors linking Berlin to the German Federal Republic, then he argued that British or American troops could not travel along the autobahn except at specific times, then that they had to use particular frequencies on their radios.

A surrender on one apparently minor point could well have led to a situation in which so many rights had been lost that the position of West Berlin itself became untenable, and Eurosceptics tend to take a comparable view of the ambitions entertained by the Brussels bureaucracy and by continental politicians. However innocuous the proposals coming from Bonn or Brussels may seem, they argue, they form part of a drive for power which Bernard Connolly, in *The Rotten Heart of Europe*, attributes both to the

cunning, crafty and fiercely nationalistic French *énarques* who will end
up running the show

and to the view supposedly held by the Bundesbank, which is that the single
currency, like the ERM before it, will be tolerable 'only with undisputed
German leadership'.[6]

As is fairly clear from the style in which Bernard Connolly writes, it is
sometimes difficult to make a clear distinction between Euroscepticism and
Europhobia. From a cultural point of view, there is something slightly ironic
about this, since the kind of argument which he and other Eurosceptics
present is closely linked to what is a very European tradition in historical
analysis and political thought. It is one which seeks to explain political
behaviour by the desire to exercise power, and was first expressed by the
Greek historian Thucydides (*c*.460-*c*.400 BC) in his *History of the Peloponnesian War*, the account of the struggle for supremacy between Athens
and Sparta which lasted from 431 BC and ended with the defeat of Athens
in 404 BC.

One of the questions which Thucydides set himself was to ask why, in
416 BC, the Athenians attacked the neutral island of Melos, conquered it,
slaughtered all the male inhabitants, and sent the women and children into
slavery. He did so in what is known as the Melian Dialogue, in Book V of
the *History of the Peloponnesian War*, where a group of Athenian envoys
explain to the representatives of the island of Melos why it is in their own
best interest to give up their neutrality and join the Athenian empire. As the
Athenians point out, it is necessary for the prestige of Athens as a maritime
power that islanders such as the Melians should not be seen as able to defy
it by remaining neutral. When the Melians object, pointing out that they are
not doing anybody any harm, and basing their claim to neutrality on what
would nowadays be called the right to self-determination, the Athenians
persist. They draw the attention of the Melians to the fact that their forces
are there in overwhelming strength, that neither the Gods nor the Spartans
are likely to come to their aid, and finally justify their conduct by the
argument that

> of the Gods we believe, and of men we know, that by a law of their nature
> wherever they can rule they will.

One of the many originalities of Thucydides as a historian lies in his
ambition to discover the laws which govern human conduct. This leads him,
in the Melian dialogue, to present one of the great war crimes of the fifth
century not with the moral indignation which Euripides showed when he
evoked it by analogy in *The Trojan Women* in 415 BC, but as an illustrative
example of why men act as they do. It is, Thucydides argues, because the

political groups to which they belong place them in situations where they cannot choose but rule. Since the exercise of power excites in those who are ruled a constant desire for rebellion and revenge, the rulers cannot give up their power without making themselves vulnerable to the hatred they have inspired. They are forced by fear to behave with a cruelty which no conscious desire to inflict suffering could possibly inspire.

There is, naturally, no question of any state in the European Union behaving as the Athenians did at Melos. One of the great achievements of the process which began with the signing of the Treaty of Paris in 1951 has been the effective outlawing of war between the states of Western Europe. But there are two strands to the objections to a single currency voiced by British Eurosceptics which have a Thucydidean note, of which the first is the view that a Franco-German condominium is consciously seeking to dominate Europe for its own ends. However sound the technical arguments put forward in favour of a single currency may be, it is alleged, the real motive is a political one, and it lies in the desire to exercise power.

This is also a view which goes hand in hand with one of the deeper insights in Thucydides: that all states reach a point in their development where the power they possess makes it impossible for them not to use it to dominate those around them. This, it is argued, is currently the case with Germany. With reunification bringing its population up to the 80 million which it had in 1914 and 1939, it cannot avoid dominating Europe, even if it does not wish to do so. The laws governing the behaviour of nation states are determined by the power given to them by their size, not the conscious intentions of their rulers.

There is nevertheless a more positive side to what becomes, when voiced by British Eurosceptics, a less morally neutral attribution of nefarious ambitions to the French and Germans. It remains, it is true, eminently Thucydidean in its presupposition that the aim of politics is the pursuit of power. But it also involves, without those expressing it always being aware of the fact, a wholly beneficial rewriting of Clausewitz's dictum that war is the continuation of politics by other means. For it is, nowadays, economics which is the pursuit of politics by other means, and the creation of wealth, an activity which I praise at greater length in the Conclusion, which has become the main object of national politics as well as of the kind of international co-operation represented by the European Union.

If the single currency goes ahead, a country wishing to adopt it must have a deficit of less than 3 per cent of its GNP. This idea is more generally and somewhat euphemistically expressed in English economic discourse by talking about the Public Deficit Borrowing Requirement. When applied to a person, as I explain in more detail later by talking about Mr Micawber, it means that someone with a net income of £30,000 a year needs to borrow another £900 a year to pay all their bills. A country wishing to satisfy the Maastricht criteria must also not have a public debt higher than 60 per cent of its GNP, an inflation rate no higher than 1.5 per cent of the average of the countries in the European Union with the lowest inflation rate (in practice, 3 per cent), and not to have devalued within the limits of the middle, 6 per cent band of the ERM over the last two years.

Late in 1996, not even Germany qualified on all four conditions, and was going to have to introduce an austerity budget to bring its deficit down from 3.6 per cent to the required 3 per cent. Belgium was in an even worse position, with a public deficit of 4.5 per cent, Spain had 6.5 per cent and Italy 7.2 per cent. France was reported as having a deficit of 5 per cent, and therefore to be in a position of risking serious disruption from trade unions if the Juppé government implemented the programme of cuts in public expenditure necessary to enable France to qualify for membership.

Ireland, Holland and Luxembourg seemed best placed. The United Kingdom, with a deficit of 4.6 per cent and a public debt of 120 per cent of its GDP, would have to make a considerable effort if it did decide that it wanted to join. Ireland, in contrast, has been one of the countries whose economic performance has shown the greatest improvement since it entered the Community in 1973. It has had a steady growth rate of 4 per cent a year, and receives £5 back from the various Community funds for every £1 which it contributes to the European budget. It was one of the countries which, when the EMS was first set up in 1978, was able to join the ± 2.5 per cent fluctuation band. Although its public debt was 84.6 per cent of its GDP in 1995, it satisfied three of the other criteria, and is one of the countries whose citizens regularly reply to enquiries about the popularity of the European Union with an enthusiastic endorsement of its achievements.

Mr Micawber's remark to David Copperfield is a useful reminder of the difference between an individual person and a nation state, as well as a convenient way of understanding in simplified terms what is meant by a percentage deficit of a country's GDP. For Mr Micawber was perfectly right, as a private citizen frequently afflicted with pecuniary embarrassment, to say, as he did

> Annual income twenty pounds, annual expenditure nineteen six, result happiness. Annual income twenty pounds, annual expenditure twenty pounds ought and six, result misery.

Because of the reputation he had acquired over the years of 'waiting for something to come up' before settling his debts, he would not have been able to find anyone to lend him the sixpence, or 0.125 per cent of his £20 a year salary which represented his annual deficit, and would indeed have been plunged in misery.

However, since nation states habitually run much larger percentage budget deficits than private individuals, a country with as low a borrowing requirement as Mr Micawber would be a shining example of the compelling virtue in the proposed transition from the ERM to a single currency. If Mr Micawber had been a nation state seeking to satisfy the Maastricht criteria, he would have been able to talk about twelve shillings, or twenty-four sixpences, as the difference between happiness and misery. Had he been alive in 1997, of course, it would have been the less poetic sixty pence, with the even less poetic two and a half pence as the equivalent of sixpence.

A more fortunately placed twentieth-century figure with an annual salary of £100,000 paying off a £60,000 mortgage would constitute the equivalent of a state having a debt which amounted to 60 per cent of its annual GDP. Such an individual would, of course, also need not to have spent £3,000 more in the current year than in the previous year, especially if living in a community whose other members were comparably frugal.

The convergence criteria set out in the Maastricht Treaty amount in practice essentially to a readiness and ability to cut your coat according to your cloth, and correspond to what Lady Thatcher – who is not, in other respects, a supporter of the European Single Currency – would have called prudent housekeeping. Since the great inflation of the 1970s and 1980s, which saw the purchasing power of the 1969 pound fall to that of about fifteen new pence, it has been seen as axiomatic that any government's first priority in managing the national economy is an ability to keep inflation down at least to under 5 per cent. This is something which a well-ordered national government can do by itself, without either joining the ERM or its equivalent, and without adopting a single currency. The convergence requirements set out in the Maastricht criteria are, in this respect, economic targets which, from a monetarist and anti-inflationist viewpoint, are good in themselves, whether one wants to join a single currency or not.

Thus if the British government had been able to stick to the equivalent of the Maastricht criteria over the last thirty years, its citizens would not have seen the exchange value of the pound fall from 11.20 Deutschmark in 1965 to 2.31 in 1995. Indeed, there are even journalists such as Auberon Waugh who maintain, perhaps not entirely seriously, that if the German bankers who are said to be likely to take the decisions about the British economy, if we do join the single currency, can maintain the purchasing value of our money as efficiently as they have done that of their own, he would much rather have them managing his affairs than his elected representatives at Westminster.

As his remark brings out, the arguments for and against the single currency are indeed political as well as economic, and are complicated by a number of factors. One of these is the general question of whether one wishes to endure the torments of what Denis Healey calls sado-monetarism in order to keep a low inflation rate. Low inflation alone does not guarantee prosperity. The period 1918–1939 was one of the most miserable of the century in economic terms, but was marked in the United Kingdom by zero inflation, if not in fact by a slight increase in the purchasing power of the pound. Periods of low inflation have tended, historically, to be periods of high unemployment, and the large number of people without jobs in countries such as France and Germany, which are at the moment making determined efforts to meet the Maastricht criteria, suggests that this may be more than just an accident. Perhaps Keynes may have been right, and inflation is the price we have to pay for a reasonable rate of employment.

The decision as to which of the two evils, unemployment or inflation, governments choose to inflict on their citizens is a political one, and the political subtext of the Maastricht convergence criteria, seen from a socialist point of view, consists of a determined attempt to keep the working class in its place by making its members perpetually terrified of losing their jobs. It is, in several senses of the word, a banker's agenda, and any government deciding to adopt it is taking a political decision. It might indeed justify this decision by the argument that only a determined effort to control inflation will produce a lasting prosperity in which everyone, in the end, will have a real job in an economy that works. But in the long run, as Keynes remarked, we are all dead, and nobody seems able to predict how long the adjustment of all fifteen member states of the European Union to the non-inflationary priorities of the Maastricht Treaty will take.

In another of the pamphlets put out by the Office for Official Publications of the European Union, *For a Social Europe*, the point is made that while Japan spends only 12 per cent of the GNP on providing health and social services for its citizens, and the United States of America 15 per cent, the average over the fifteen member countries of the European Union is 22 per cent. This figure is not presented as a justification for the obvious desire of the Maastricht criteria to limit public expenditure so that Europe can become more competitive in the global market. It is nevertheless there as part of the subtext to the creation of a European Single Currency whose primary characteristics will be its competitiveness and stability.

While these criticisms of the Maastricht criteria come essentially from the left, it is not unusual to hear British right-wing Eurosceptics interpreting both the idea of a single currency and the term 'economic and monetary union' in a particularly rigorous way in order to strengthen their case against Great Britain giving up the pound in exchange for the Euro. For when the Eurosceptics give their very hawkish interpretation of the Maastricht Treaty, they maintain that the full realisation of economic and monetary union will mean far more than the disappearance of the Austrian schilling, the Belgian franc, the British pound, the Danish and Swedish krøner, the Dutch guilder, the Finnish markka, the French franc, the Deutschmark, the Greek drachma, the Portuguese escudo and the Spanish peseta and their consequent replacement by the Euro.

If the words 'economic and monetary union' really mean what they say, argue the Eurosceptics, and if the comparison with the United States of America is one which can be taken seriously, all citizens of the European Union, and all businesses in the fifteen countries, will pay the same rate of direct as well as of indirect taxation, as well as paying the same social security contributions, and receiving the same benefits. They will thus cease, from an economic point of view, to be citizens of their own country. They will belong instead to a vast conglomerate whose decisions they will never be able to influence either by the ballot box or by membership of a trade union, professional organisation, or independent pressure group. Neither, since the membership of the European Single Currency will require a state to hand over to the European Central Bank a large proportion of its gold and currency reserves, will a country which has joined have any real control over its national financial assets.

The basis for the Eurosceptic view that a single currency will involve sweeping changes of this kind is in the argument that if a particular country in the European Union were to allow companies based on its territory to pay a low rate of corporation tax, this would give it an unacceptable advantage over one where rates are higher. Companies in a low tax economy can afford to reduce their profit margins, and so produce goods more cheaply than their competitors. They can therefore pay higher wages in order to attract the most highly qualified and productive workers, and thus lengthen their already existing economic lead. If the country in which they are situated also imposes lower direct taxes on its citizens, this will give it yet another advantage in the competition for scarce, highly-qualified labour. Citizens paying income tax at a lower rate will have more disposable income to invest. They will tend to do so in the more efficient companies situated on their own territory, providing these companies with more research and development funds to increase their efficiency and make them even more competitive.

The only way in which such discrepancies can be avoided, and the principle of fair competition essential to articles 85 and 86 of the Treaty of Rome maintained, argue the Eurosceptics, is by the introduction in all fifteen countries of the same rates of direct as well as indirect taxation. This, they continue, will inevitably involve a loss of national sovereignty, in that countries will then really have no control over their national economies. It will also, perhaps more importantly, mean the disappearance of the traditional right of the citizens in a parliamentary democracy to pay only those taxes which their freely elected representatives have voted to introduce.

Even if, as would still be the case, the money coming from taxes paid by British citizens continued to be paid into the British treasury, there would be no sense in which these citizens could be seen as having voted for the taxes which produced it. The decisions as to the level and system of taxation would have been decided elsewhere, by a group of bankers whose main concern is the relationship between the Euro and other international currencies such as the dollar, the yen or the Swiss franc. One of the basic ideas of European democracy would then have totally disappeared. The only thing that mattered would be the competitivity of the European economy, on which the value of the Euro would depend, in world financial markets.

The Eurosceptics back up this argument by pointing to the example of the United States economy, where the most important and immediately perceptible of personal taxes, that of direct tax on individual income, is uniform throughout the fifty states, as is also the equally important tax on company profits. Any taxes imposed by the individual states, they point out, are relatively small both in their impact and in the revenue which they produce, and they argue that the achievement of economic and monetary union would, as far as the member states of the European Union were concerned, give France or Italy no more control over their own economic policy than California or Texas have in North America. This would, in their view, not only have the disadvantage of depriving the citizens of France and Italy of the right to pay only those taxes which their freely elected members of parliament had decided to impose. It would also be very difficult, on purely practical grounds, to impose the same type of income tax on the citizens of countries with such long and different traditions as the United Kingdom and France, and even if there were no other objections to the creation of a European Single Currency, they regard this one as totally unsurmountable.

The supporters of a European Single Currency point out in reply that the comparison with the United States is, in this respect, quite misleading. Because they have a common language, and in spite of the cultural differences separating states such as Mississippi and Manhattan, something very close to a common culture, Americans have traditionally moved about a great deal to find work. The tendency of Europeans, in contrast, to stay in their own country means that much of the argument about the need for a uniform rate of income tax falls by the wayside. There is no need to tempt workers to stay in Great Britain by allowing them to pay a lower rate of tax than in Germany, because not many of them would want to go to work in Germany anyway. It would therefore, they argue, be perfectly possible for the different states in the European Union to have different rates of income tax, decided by their own parliament, as well as different contribution rates of payment for health and social security and different levels of benefit.

The threat to national sovereignty is, they maintain, much exaggerated by the Eurosceptics, even though one of the most persuasive of the advocates for a European Single Currency, Christopher Johnson, admits that

> If the single market is to prosper, the UK may have to agree to qualified majority voting on some tax matters, if only to prevent deposits draining out of British banks, as they have out of German banks into Luxembourg and other tax havens.

It is true that he offers a reassuring rider to this when he then writes

> No country wants to surrender its fiscal independence, but in this case some pooling of sovereignty would be to the UK's advantage. Majority voting on one or two specific taxes would have only a marginal impact of total UK tax revenue.[7]

The implication of his remark is that Westminster would still take the major decisions on tax as far as the citizens of the United Kingdom were concerned, at the same time as we all continued to benefit from the economic advantages which, in Christopher Johnson's view, a European Single Currency cannot fail to bring with it.

One of these is the very basic one of no longer needing to pay somebody to change your pounds into francs, or your drachmas back into pounds at the end of your Greek holiday. The total saving in transaction costs from one European currency into another could, Mr Johnson suggests, be as high as 0.33 per cent of the total GDP of all fifteen countries in the European Union. This would amount, for the United Kingdom, to some £2.5 billion, and for the European Union as a whole £25 billion. The European Commission itself, as Charles Goodhart mentions in his article 'EMU: A Future That Works' in the December 1995 issue of *Prospect*, is even more optimistic. It gives the savings in transaction costs as 0.5 per cent of the total GDP, though Mr Goodhart himself draws attention to a purely practical problem inseparable from the creation of a European Single Currency when he comments that the current value of the Irish punt is 0.808628 of an ECU, and adds

> Normally currency reforms simply shift the decimal point. Not in this case. Trying to change all the paper currency and coins of all the member states into a user-friendly European form is going to be so difficult, so expensive and so wildly unpopular that it could endanger the whole.[8]

The main advantage of a single currency would nevertheless be more in the area of macro-economics than in the advantage of no longer feeling that you are being ripped off by the banks and made to pay an extra 5 per cent surcharge on your continental holiday before you even leave home. Goods and services would circulate even more freely than they do at present, and there would be corresponding economies of size in research, development and production costs. Inflation would be more firmly under control, with a corresponding benefit to the level of investment.

At the moment, one of the great disincentives to investment, especially in a country such as Britain, is the fear that any profits from the dividends offered by shares are simply going to be eaten up by inflation. This leads potential investors to behave in what is in fact a self-defeating way, both for themselves and for the economy as a whole. When they keep their savings in a Building Society or a National Savings Ordinary Account on the grounds that 'their money is safe there' and they can 'always get at it when they want', they do in fact suffer far more from the effects of inflation than those who have had the courage to go into equities.

These more timid investors are nevertheless unlikely to change their behaviour unless and until they are assured that inflation will remain low enough for them to make a profit from a more productive investment in industry. An increase in private investment patterns of this kind would help to bring the economic performance of the European Union up to that of the United States or Japan, both of which have a much higher savings ratio than a country such as Great Britain or Italy, and are correspondingly more prosperous.

The existence of a single currency, as the experience of the United States in the 1970s and early 1980s shows, is no protection against inflation. What is new in the way a European Single Currency is being planned is that it is linked with a general change in economic policy expressly designed to limit inflation. Basic to the convergence criteria set out in the Maastricht Treaty as a precondition for a country to join the European Single Currency is the idea that parliamentary democracies are peculiarly vulnerable to inflation, and ought therefore to be protected against themselves.

What the supporters of a European Single Currency implicitly maintain, in this respect, is that there is always the temptation, for a party in power in a democracy, to try to win the next election by giving a sudden boost to the economy in order to win more votes by creating a 'feel-good factor'. Since one of the principal ways in which they do this is by reducing interest rates, the only effect of this barely disguised form of bribery, in the long run and quite frequently in the short run as well, is to encourage inflation by giving the electors money to buy goods which they cannot really afford, the Maastricht criteria have as their obvious and prime aim that of discouraging governments from behaving in such a profligate and irresponsible manner. If the government of a particular country continues to behave in the improvident way that many of them have done in the past, thus failing to discourage inflation in the way that their duty dictates that they should, they will not be allowed to join in a European Single Currency, and will therefore miss out on the benefits which it will bring with it.

This underlying ambition of the Maastricht Treaty to make member countries of the European Union behave in a way which is seen as more responsible than their conduct in the past is even more clearly visible in the proposed arrangements for running the single currency once it is established. The European Monetary Institute, as Christopher Johnson observes in chapter 4 of *In With the Euro, Out With the Pound*, is best seen as 'the forerunner' of the Independent European Central Bank, due to come into existence in 1999 in order to administer the single currency. His description of the membership, functions and responsibilities of this bank is consequently a good indication of what the European Single Currency will mean in terms of the transfer of economic power from the individual states in the European Union to a central institution.

This bank will have an Executive Board of six permanent members, together with a representative of the central bank of each of the fifteen member states. It will not therefore be possible for elected politicians to influence the decisions which the bank takes with regard to interest rates. The general macro-economic policy of the Union will thus become the responsibility of bankers, a reflection of the criticism expressed earlier that elected politicians, and more especially politicians seeking to be re-elected, have been too improvident in the past to be trusted with the guardianship of the European Single Currency. There is, in this argument, a distinct echo of Clemenceau's remark that war is too important a matter to be left to generals. The performance of both French and British generals during the 1914–1918 war suggests that Clemenceau might have been right, and that if one's prime concern in managing a currency is to ensure that it does not lose its value, bankers may well do a better job than elected politicians. This is certainly the view taken in the United States of America, where the chairman of the Federal Reserve Bank, currently Alan Greenspan, decides the lending rate for all banks across the United States without being required to consult any politician at all.

The insistence that the budget deficit of a country wishing to qualify for entry into the European Single Currency must not exceed 3 per cent of the GNP suggests that the policy of the Independent European Central Bank will be firmly anti-Keynesian. There will be no boosting of the economy by deficit financing, and in that respect the accusation that present developments in the European Union involve 'bringing socialism in again by the back door' are again not very well founded. Neither does there seem to be much evidence to support the other accusation most frequently made by

British Eurosceptics that the creation of a European Single Currency will confirm the position of Germany not only as the strongest member of the European Union but also the one which dominates its activities.

Germany is bound to remain the strongest member of the European Union. With 80 million inhabitants, its geographical position in the centre of Europe, its tradition of hard work, applied science and good industrial relationships, this is something which cannot be avoided. The only alternative is to put into practice François Mauriac's remark that he is so fond of Germany that he would like there to be two of it. But as Christopher Johnson argues, the number of people involved in running the Independent Central European Bank will make it very difficult either for the six permanent members or for the representative of any one single bank to dominate proceedings. This, he adds, is 'a fact which could explain why the Bundesbank drags its feet about European Monetary Union from time to time'[9] and it is a mistake for the British to think that they are the only people to have reservations about the creation of a European Single Currency. If Germany really did want to dominate Europe, as distinct from being a major player in its councils, it would be better advised to stick with the Deutschmark and make everybody else align their currency on its performance.

All this, however, like most aspects of the proposed European Single Currency, is highly speculative. Indeed, to write about it as I am doing, in April 1997, is rather like placing oneself in the position of a sports reporter required to submit copy of his account of a football match twenty minutes before the final whistle has been blown. It is by no means certain what control a nation state in the European Union would retain over the details of its economic policy if and when a European Single Currency is established, and no details have yet been provided of the level at which the various countries taking part in it would join.[10] The decision of Winston Churchill, in April 1925, to go back to the gold standard with the pound at too high a rate was a major contributory cause to the great depression of the 1930s, and it has already been noted how the decision to enter the ERM in 1990 with the pound at 2.93 Deutschmark led to its ignominious exit two years later.

It is clear that a country going into the single currency would not be able to decide general interest rates, but would receive in return a welcome relief from having to worry about balance of payments problems. West Virginia is not the most prosperous state in the United States, but it does not have to keep worrying about the effect on the dollar in the pocket of its inhabitants or its balance of trade with the other 49 states. All that happens is that wages there are lower than in more prosperous states such as Texas or California. West Virginia can, within the limits imposed by the United States system, decide what to do economically without running the risk of being blown off course by a balance of payments crisis.

Member states of the European Union will, if the European Single Currency is created, be in a similar position of not having to worry about their currency losing its official value as a result of an imbalance of trade. The Euro will, naturally, have a different purchasing power between countries rather as the pound buys more in Penrith than it does either in central London or on the island of Mull. The individual states of the European Union will also have greater power over what happens economically within their borders than is possessed either by the individual states which make up the United States or by the provinces in Canada. Indeed, it could even be argued that the creation of a single currency would require the member states of the European Union to make greater use of fiscal policy in the organisation of their economic life, and would thus give them a greater independence than the Eurosceptics think would be possible.

Thus a state wishing to increase public spending, or to introduce a fairly high minimum wage, would still be able to do so. This would have a potentially inflationary effect inseparable from a general increase in the purchasing power of its inhabitants, and might thus lead commercial banks to move their money out of that country. But the freedom of that particular country to increase taxes, which would at that point become a necessity, would still leave it with a series of economic choices. It could choose to be a state with a high level of public spending, so long as this was counterbalanced by an increase in taxes. Alternatively, a country could decide, as the United Kingdom has decided by refusing to implement the Social Chapter, to be a relatively low wage economy in which the balance of power lies with employers rather than the workforce. This could, in the essentially capitalist system which will continue to be the model for the European Union, lead firms from other member countries to establish their businesses there, on the grounds that their wage bill would be lower and their profits higher.

The situation would naturally change if the Social Chapter were to become mandatory, and even more if the decision to do this were to be accompanied by a Directive establishing the 48-hour working week, perhaps accompanied by a minimum wage, as obligatory throughout the Union. At the moment, and certainly in the United Kingdom, a 48-hour working week is a theoretical concept rather than an effective reality. Employers cannot require employees to work more than 48 hours without paying overtime. But there is nothing to prevent them from giving preferential treatment to employees prepared to make an extra, unpaid effort, especially when consideration is given to drawing up a redundancy list. This is particularly the case with salaried employees in the finance and service industries, as well as in the professions such as accountancy or the law. The remark allegedly made by the American employer who told the workforce that anyone not happy at the idea of working on a Saturday afternoon need not bother to turn up on Sunday morning may still reflect transatlantic rather than European practices. Increased competition from the Far East and Pacific Rim economies may nevertheless give it a world-wide applicability, thus calling into question the whole issue of the sustainability of the Social Chapter.

The full implementation of a Directive establishing a 48-hour week would also do more than contradict the essentially anti-inflationary strategy of the Maastricht criteria. The most immediate effect of the reduction of the working week has, in the past, been an increase in overtime, creating higher wages, higher costs for industry, greater purchasing power and higher inflation. There would also be the political question of what would then happen to a country which refused to implement a decision which had presumably been reached by a qualified majority in the Council of Ministers. There are few precedents for a genuine implementation of the Gaullist principle of national independence embodied in the Luxembourg compromise of 1966, but this might be one of them.

Conclusion

Dr Johnson's remark that a man is seldom so innocently employed as when he is making money provides what might rather grandly be called the philosophical background for the process of European unification which began in 1951 with the signature of the Treaty of Paris. The initial desire to avoid a fourth war between France and Germany has been so fully realised as to have been virtually forgotten as a conscious aim. What has arisen in its place is the increasing recognition that what should really accompany the unification of the various states of Western Europe is an activity at which Europeans have become even more adept than they were in the past in making war against one another. That of making money.

This is a highly laudable objective, and the steady contemplation of the desire to increase the wealth of the citizens of Europe, and which provides the driving force for the European Union today, is one of the great intellectual pleasures of the late twentieth century. Few events in history give one greater faith in one's fellow human beings than this now virtually universal realisation that the main role of the nation state has become that of devising means to enable its citizens to grow richer. There may be disagreement about how best to do this. Differences about the right economic policy to pursue can sometimes be quite vigorously expressed. But there is no doubt about the aim which the state now sees as its duty to pursue: that of creating wealth efficiently and devising means for it to be redistributed fairly. When one recalls what some states, and some international organisations, have tried to do in the past, it is a staggering achievement.

Such a replacement presupposes, of course, that the money created by the lucky and skilful is going to be redistributed in some way or other to the unlucky and the unskilled, to those unfortunate enough not to have been blessed by the combination of good genes and a favourable environment which have enabled their fellow citizens to create the wealth to be taken in taxes. It is this idea of redistributing wealth which lies behind such characteristically European projects as the Social Chapter, just as it was the fundamental ambition of the European Community to make people richer which inspired the elimination of customs duties and the constant attempt to make agriculture and industry more efficient by free and fair competition.

This insistence on the importance of money involves no disparagement of the thinkers who have tried to build the idea of Europe on the intellectual inheritance provided by the Greek passion for abstract thought and unrestricted intellectual argument. Neither is there any inconsistency between the ambition to make money and the idea that there is a common European social heritage stemming from the Roman concept of a law common to all citizens and standing above party groupings, private interests, or even the state itself. The thinkers who have seen a way to European unity in the various concepts of Christian spirituality can, indeed, point out that it was Christianity which inspired the cathedrals of the Middle Ages, much of the art of the Renaissance, as well as the language of the versions of the Bible provided in the native tongues of the Europeans at the time of the Reformation. The fact nevertheless remains that there is one characteristic common to all the attempts to unify Europe from the top, as it were, and which have taken their starting point in its intellectual and spiritual achievements rather than in the idea of making money. They have all failed.

It is again significant, in this respect, that it was money which lay at the origin of one of the most important contributions which the British made to the European heritage. For it was in the civil war of the English parliamentarians against Charles I, in the seventeenth century, that the idea of subjecting the King to the authority of parliament and to the rule of law was put to the test and triumphed on the field of battle. It was from the peaceful revolution of 1688, in which James II was dismissed and replaced by William and Mary, sovereigns whose religion and political ideas were more acceptable to the wealthy land-owners, parliamentarians and churchmen of the time, that there grew and developed the specifically European idea of the contract theory of government. But in both cases, the original driving force came from the desire of those who called the King's authority into question to protect their wealth against what they saw as his unlawful attempt to take and use it for his own purposes.

The nobles, lawyers, land-owners and merchants who carried out the revolutions of the seventeenth century also developed a set of ideas which inspired the whole eighteenth-century movement known as the Enlightenment, and which led to the American Revolution of 1776 as well as to the French Revolution of 1789. When, in 1825, Thomas Jefferson founded the University of Virginia, and had carved above its portals the words

Here, we are not afraid to follow truth wherever it may lead, nor to tolerate any error so long as reason is left free to combat it.

he was expressing a European ideal, but one born in England from the desire of the parliamentarians of the seventeenth century to stop the King getting his hands on their money.

There have, naturally, been other thinkers, from the seventeenth century onwards, who have looked for a way in which the Europeans could unite. But like the other intellectual and spiritual achievements of Europeans, such as the rationalism of Descartes, the idealism of Kant, or the doctrine of the rights of man, these have all been perfectly consistent with the desire to create wealth. Men such as Jean Monnet or Robert Schuman did indeed see these spiritual and intellectual ideals as Europe's crowning glory, the principal reasons why it was so important to unite Europe, in order that this inheritance might be preserved. But the actions which they and others like them took were all based upon the presupposition that it was money – or, if one prefers a grander phrase, economic prosperity – which provided the foundation for this inheritance.

The career of the most important of the founding fathers of the present-day European Union, Jean Monnet, is in this respect an illustration of why the movement towards European unity which he inspired succeeded, when so many earlier projects had failed. He had begun his career as a salesman for the family firm of cognac distillers. In the first world war, he had represented France in the inter-allied commissions responsible for sharing economic resources. Between the wars, he had worked as Assistant General Secretary to the League of Nations the unsuccessful forerunner of the present United Nations. In this role, he had arranged international loans for Romania and Poland, and helped to reorganise the Chinese railway system. During the second world war, he had worked in the Victory Programme of President Roosevelt, and signed the lend-lease agreements between France and the United States. He became the first President of the European Coal and Steel Community, a fitting tribute to his practical grasp of the realities of business life which led him to begin by so apparently mundane a proposal as the dismantling of all customs duties for coal and steel.

Notes

1 HISTORY

1 For a checklist of the member states, together with their dates of accession and the development of what began as the ECSC, see the Chronology on p. ix.

2 A more detailed account of the economic aspects of the ECSC can be found in Martin J. Dedman, *The Origins and Development of the European Union, 1951–1995*, Routledge, London and New York, 1996, pp. 60–9.

3 For the German objectives between 1914 and 1918, see the German historian Fritz Fischer's *German War Aims in the First World War*, Oxford University Press, Oxford, 1967, and his analysis of the ambition of the Second Reich to annex Belgium and Luxembourg, reduce France to a satellite state from which all British goods would be excluded and which had no army to defend itself, and transfer control of France's and Belgium's African colonies to Germany.

4 The more unattractive a régime, the more likely will it be to attack its neighbours on a day which they wish to devote to more peaceful pursuits. It was, as will be seen, on the eve of Yom Kippur, or the Day of Atonement, that the Muslim régimes of the Middle East made their last attempt, in October 1973, to destroy Israel by force of arms. It was on Sunday, 1 August 1914, in other words on a Bank Holiday weekend, that Germany declared war on France and Russia. Hitler precipitated the second world war by invading Poland on Friday, 1 September 1939, again at the beginning of a weekend, and giving the United Kingdom no choice but to declare war on Sunday, 3 September. It was on Saturday, 21 June 1941 that Hitler invaded the Soviet Union, and the film *From Here to Eternity* makes a point of showing the time on all the clocks as 07.50 on Sunday, 7 December 1941 to mark the 'day of infamy' of the Japanese attack on Pearl Harbour. It was on Sunday, 4 November 1956 that Soviet tanks moved into Budapest to crush the attempts of the Hungarians to assert their independence against the USSR. It was on the night of Sunday, 13 August 1961 that the East Germans closed the border between East and West Berlin, thus taking the first step in the building of the Berlin Wall. On a happier note, it was in the afternoon of Sunday, 27 October 1962 that the announcement reached Great Britain that the Soviet Union had agreed to withdraw its missiles from Cuba. The event was seen as sufficiently important to justify interrupting the popular police programme *Z Cars*. Whatever reservations one may have about moves to a Federal Europe, it is unlikely that these reservations will be strengthened by the

gratuitous interruption of one's peaceful weekend activities by aggressive military moves.

5 Details of de Gaulle's press conference are given in Volume three of Jean Lacouture's biography of de Gaulle, *Le Souverain*, Seuil, Paris, 1986 and the issue is very well discussed in P.M.H. Bell's admirable *France and Britain, 1940–1994. The Long Separation*, Longman, London, 1997. Norah Beloff's *The General Says No*, Penguin, London, 1963 remains an excellent analysis.

6 See Pierre Gerbet, *La Construction de l'Europe*, Seuil, Paris, 1983, pp. 256–7.

7 It is of course true that the Nazi movement, the most virulent expression of totalitarianism in Western Europe, arose in Germany, the homeland of Kant and Lessing, and was led by Hitler, a fellow countryman of Mozart. Nazism was an essentially revolutionary movement, and was thus different in its aims as well as its nature from the essentially conservative form which totalitarianism took with Franco and Salazar, or with the Greek colonels.

2 ORGANISATION AND POWERS

1 Published by Faber and Faber, London, and presenting a number of economic arguments against a common European currency which are enlivened by phrases such as 'the politically subservient and stridently anglophobe French press' (p. 295), 'the near gangsters in Italian politics' (p. 132), 'Joao de Deus Pinto, the Satanic-featured Portuguese Foreign Minister', (p.130) as well as by the view that Mrs Thatcher's resignation as Prime Minister in November 1989 was the result of 'murderous intention by the Commission and Britain's "partners" in Europe' (p. 72).

Bernard Connolly's main argument, that 'the cynicism of the French technocrats, traitors to their own people, and the arrogant, overbearing, menacing zeal of the German federalists, not to mention the grandiose ambitions of Helmut Kohl, remain on a collision course' (p.392) is examined in more detail in the passage on Thucydides in Chapter 5. In Bernard Connolly's view, this 'collision course' is quite capable of leading to another war between France and Germany, and thus defeating the main political objective inspiring the creation of the ECSC of 1951.

2 Quoted in Dennis Swann, *The Economics of the Common Market*, Penguin, London, 1970, sixth edition, 1984, p. 7.

3 See *The Single Market*, Office for Official Publications of the European Communities, Luxembourg, 1995, p. 29.

4 *The ABC of Community Law*, Office for Official Publications of the European Communities, Luxembourg, 1994, p. 24.

5 *The Penguin Companion to the European Union*, Penguin, London, 1995, revised edition, 1996, p. 94.

6 See Timothy Bainbridge and Anthony Teasdale, *The Penguin Companion to the European Union*, Penguin, London, 1995, revised edition, 1996, p. 213.

7 See *The ABC of Community Law*, Office for Official Publications of the European Communities, Luxembourg, 1994, p.28.

8 *The Economics of the Common Market*, Penguin, London, 1990, p. 55.

9 Lord Cockfield, *The European Union. Creating the Single Market*, Wiley Chancery Law, London, 1994, pp. 95–6.

10 A list of the meetings, together with a brief summary of the matters dealt with, can be found on pp. 173–6 of Timothy Bainbridge and Anthony Teasdale, *The*

Penguin Companion to the European Union, Penguin, London, 1995, revised edition, 1996.

11 See *The Civil Service Handbook* for 1996, which gives the figure of 516,893 permanent civil servants employed on 1 April 1995. However, according to *Whitaker's Almanac* for 1996, 65 per cent of the work previously done by the Civil Service is now carried out by agencies, and *The Civil Service Handbook* gives a total of 345,342 people employed by all agencies on 1 April 1996.

Figures such as these should be handled with considerable caution. Different countries classify different professions differently, and the fact that France is described as having two and a half million civil servants is explained partly by the fact that all teachers in the public sector are employed by the state, and not by local authorities or individual universities, while a good deal of the work done by locally paid administrators in the United Kingdom is performed by civil servants in France.

3 BASIC PRINCIPLES

1 *The Economics of the Common Market*, Penguin Books, London, 1990, p. 98.

2 Quoted in Stephen George, *An Awkward Partner. Britain in the European Community*, Oxford University Press, Oxford, 1990, p.26.

3 See Pascal Fontaine, *Europe in Ten Points*, European Documentation, Luxembourg, 1995, p. 31. For an explanation of the term 'directive', see p. 38 of Chapter 2.

4 I do not myself believe these figures, and would base my own plans on them only after having consulted a responsible official from the Customs and Excise Department. In practice, however, I understand that checks are very rarely made, and am unable to explain two phenomena: why, since so many English people go abroad and can bring back so much drink and tobacco at so low a price, the European Union is not more popular; and why supermarkets and wine stores in the United Kingdom still sell so much alcohol at the price required by the current rate of excise duty.

5 See Lord Cockfield, *The European Union. Creating the Single Market*, Wiley Chancery Law, London, 1994, p. 79.

6 See Klaus-Dieter Borchardt, *The ABC of Community Law*, European Documentation, Luxembourg, 1994, p. 60.

7 I would not personally try to do this, especially in France. A number of my former students from the French Department at the University of Leeds have sat the *Agrégation d'anglais*, and been failed by the examiners at the oral on the grounds that the English which they spoke, as native speakers of the language, was not up to French standards. A struggle is going on between the principles theoretically accepted by the European Union and the practices actually followed by the established bureaucracies of continental Europe. It is by no means certain that the latter will lose, especially in France. However prestigious a job you may obtain with a Paris-based French firm of chartered accountants, you will still need to get a resident's permit; and this you will obtain only if you can produce a recently receipted bill for electricity consumed in the Paris area.

8 See *La Politique Européenne de Concurrence*, XXVe Rapport sur la politique de concurrence, Commission Européenne, Brussels, 1995, pp. 22, 50 and 51.

9 Published by Oxford University Press, 1990. Lord Cockfield, in his *The*

European Union. Constructing the Single Market, Wiley Chancery Law, London, 1994, describes Britain as 'a reluctant bride'.
10 Alain Peyrefitte, *C'Était de Gaulle*, Seuil, Paris, 1994, pp. 158–9.
11 *The Rotten Heart of Europe. The Dirty War for Europe's Money*, Faber and Faber, London, 1995, pp. 198 and 207.

4 CONTESTED PRACTICES

1 J-M. Jeanneney, *L'Économie Française depuis 1967*, Paris, 1989, quoted by P.M.H. Bell, *France and Britain 1940–1994. The Long Separation*, Longman, London, 1997, p.240.
2 'Hopping Mad', *Prospect*, February 1997, pp. 12–13.
3 *The Rotten Heart of Europe*, Faber and Faber, London, 1995, p. 201.
4 See Timothy Bainbridge and Anthony Teasdale, *The Penguin Companion to the European Union*, Penguin, London, 1996, p. 29.
5 Quoted from Stephen George, *An Awkward Partner, Britain in the European Community* Oxford University Press, Oxford, 1991, p.194.
6 For a full discussion of the issue, see Sarah Helm, 'Europe's Chocolate Wars', in the March 1996 issue of the magazine *Prospect*. *The Daily Telegraph* is also a good source of examples, and takes the robustly Eurosceptical line encapsulated in its leading article of 30 August 1996 which recommended 'a new Act of Parliament which could list those fields of policy that do not affect any other country – such as health, immigration, taxation and industrial relations – and explicitly affirm the supremacy of parliament over them'. 'Any European directive covering these areas', it added, 'could then be seen as advisory'.
7 For a full discussion of this issue, see Clive H. Church and David Phinnemore, *European Union and the European Community. A Handbook and Commentary on the Post-Maastricht Treaties*, Harvester Wheatsheaf, London, 1994, p. 143.
8 The articles of the Social Chapter concern: freedom of movement; employment and remuneration; improvement of living and working conditions; social protection; freedom of association and collective bargaining; vocational training; equal treatment for men and women; information, consultation and participation of workers; health protection and safety at the workplace; protection of children and adolescents; the rights of elderly persons; the rights of disabled persons.
    The Social Chapter should be distinguished from the Social Charter, which is the creation of the Council of Europe, an organisation which is quite distinct from the European Union. Although the two documents have comparable aims, with both seeking to improve the status and working conditions for employees, the Charter is a purely voluntary document, with no machinery for requiring the countries which have signed it to enforce its provisions. The Social Chapter, in contrast, was given a legal basis in the Maastricht Treaty of December 1991, with only the United Kingdom abstaining, and thus obtaining an opt out which allowed it not to apply its provisions. Apart from the United Kingdom, it is therefore possible for an organisation to appeal to the Court of Justice of the European Union against any country which does not enforce it.
9 See the entry 'Contributions and Receipts' in Timothy Bainbridge and Anthony Teasdale, *The Penguin Companion to the European Union*, Penguin, London 1996, p. 83. The smallness of France's contribution is explicable by the fact that she imports very little food from 'Third Countries'.

5   CURRENCIES AND POWER

1   See *The Rotten Heart of Europe*, Faber and Faber, London, 1995, footnote to p. 58, where Connolly writes:

> Anyone stupid enough to behave in this way (instead of taking a credit card or a cash card) might also be stupid enough to listen to what Leon Brittan or Roy Jenkins has to say about EMU and the Single Currency; surely no one else would. And even the tortures inflicted by money-changers on such mythical hapless souls would amount, in the aggregate, to utter insignificance compared with the undoubted costs – in unstable inflation, cyclical variations in unemployment, permanent reduced productivity, employment and real incomes – that a single currency would bring.

2   See Christopher Johnson, *In With the Euro, Out with the Pound. The Single Currency for Britain*, Penguin, London, 1996, pp. 22–4.
3   The question is discussed at length in the articles collected by Paul Templeton in *The European Currency Crisis*, Probus Publishing Company, Cambridge and Chicago, Illinois, 1993. See, especially, the contribution by Robin Leigh-Pemberton, Governor of the Bank of England at the time. For an entirely different view, see Bernard Connolly, *The Rotten Heart of Europe*, Faber and Faber, London, 1995.
4   Templeton, op. cit., pp. 10 and 222.
5   For a study of some of these ideas, see Sven Papcke's' essay 'Who Needs European Identity?' in *The Idea of Europe. Problems of National and Transnational Identity*, edited by Brian Nelson and others, Berg Publishers, Oxford, 1992. For further considerations on the intellectual unity of Europe, see the Conclusion on p. 103.
6   *The Rotten Heart of Europe*, Faber and Faber, London, 1995, pp. 73 and 103.

   The *énarques* are senior French civil servants trained at the École Nationale d' Administration (ENA), established in 1945 by joint agreement between Charles de Gaulle and the then leader of the French Communist Party, Maurice Thorez. Unlike British or American civil servants, *énarques* frequently enter national politics, and prove very successful in attaining high office. Valéry Giscard d'Estaing (President from 1974 to 1981) went to l'ENA. So, too, did Jacques Chirac, elected President in 1996, together with his current Prime Minister, Alain Juppé, the Justice Minister, Jacques Toubon and the former President of the European Commission, Jacques Delors. Before beginning his term as the longest serving President of the Commission (1985–1995), Jacques Delors was Economics and Finance Minister in the Socialist government appointed by François Mitterrand in 1981.

   For more details about l'ENA, see Philip Thody and Howard Evans, *Faux Amis and Key Words. A Dictionary Guide to French Language, Culture and Society through Lookalikes and Confusables*, Athlone Press, London, 1985.

7   *In With the Euro, Out With the Pound. The Single Currency for Britain*, Penguin, London, 1996, p. 114.
8   *Prospect*, December 1993, p. 72. Mr Goodhart's article is one of the most lucid and useful accounts of the nature and problems of a European Single Currency available.
9   *In With the Euro, Out With the Pound, The Single Currency for Britain*, Penguin, London, 1996, p. 76.

10 According to the Maastricht Treaty, this was to be based on their level in the ERM. However, since the Maastricht Treaty was signed, there have been so many movements with the ERM that this is a very inadequate guide as to what will actually be decided.

Suggestions for further reading

The Penguin Companion to the European Union, by Timothy Bainbridge and Anthony Teasdale, Penguin, London, revised edition 1996, has an excellent bibliography. So, too, does Martin Dedman's *The Origins and Development of the European Union*, Routledge, London, 1995. There is also a good bibliography of books on Community law in Klaus-Dieter Borchardt, *The ABC of Community Law*, Publications of the European Community, Luxembourg, 1993. Publications put out by the Office for Official Publications of the European Union, whose headquarters are in Luxembourg, are available in London from:

Jean Monnet House,
8 Store Gate,
London SW1P 3AT.

In addition to the books quoted in the notes, students will find useful accounts of the workings and nature of the European Union in

Barav, A. (ed.) *Commentary of the EEC Treaty and the Single European Act*, Clarendon Press, Oxford, 1993.

Drost, Harry, *What's What and Who's Who in Europe*, Cassell, London, 1993.

El-Agraa, Ali, (ed.) *Britain Within the European Community*, Macmillan, London, 1983.

George, Stephan, *Politics and Policy in the European Community*, Oxford University Press, Oxford, 1992.

Lasok, D. and Bridge, J.W., *The Law and Institutions of the European Union*, Butterworths, London, regularly updated.

Urwin, Derek, *The Community of Europe: A History of European Integration Since 1945*, Longman, London, 1991.

Weigall, David and Stirk, Peter (eds) *The Origins and Development of the European Union*, Leicester University Press, Leicester,1992.

Index